(Happy Birthday!)
Megan
O'Neill

Everything I Know

Lessons for Life, Love, and Laughter

Megan O'Neill

As always, for EDM, who taught me everything I know.

ACKNOWLEDGMENTS

To Papa, for supplying me with the best memories of my life, the knowledge of how to tell a story, my love of words, my taste in music, the little I know about golf, help with homework when I needed it, laughter, what it means to be loved unconditionally, and lots of wonderful days just spending time together. I miss you.

To my mom, for being the best; to Michael, for always being there; to Natalie, Nico, and Bella, for being the greatest cousins in the world; to Anna Marie, Alyssa, and Sarah-Lynn, who counted as a few extra granddaughters and honorary cousins. And of course, to the usual list of suspects for love and encouragement and all those good things. You know who you are.

Everything I Know

Lessons for Life, Love, and Laughter

prologue.
how to tell a story

Hollywood thinks it's so original. Take a man who had children of his own, marry him to a woman who has children of *her* own, and you have a brand-new kind of family, a "blended" family, something that people weren't all that familiar with, and have those children get along spectacularly, with very little squabbling among the siblings – who consider themselves siblings, despite no blood relation – and wow! What a fun show!

Well, once upon a time, in Aliquippa, Pennsylvania, far before this particular plotline hit the airwaves on the small screen, this was a scenario that wasn't just the imagination of some television producer.

This was real life.

Eleuterio Marocco was a stonemason who came to the United States from Rome, Italy, passing through Ellis Island with thousands upon thousands of immigrants. He settled in Logstown, Pennsylvania, a tiny section of a tiny town in a tiny county. With his first wife – a woman whose name Marocco family lore has forgotten, a woman known only as "The Lady from Greensburg" - he had two sons: Danny and Bobby. Danny would later drown in an attempt to save a friend, and Bobby would be wounded in World War II, and die of those injuries on a hospital boat.

Next, Eleuterio would marry Theresa Piroli, with whom he would have more children: James, Gloria, Domenica (called "Mamie," or "Tootsie"), the daughter who would become known as "Eleanor-who-died" in conversation, for reasons which will soon become clear, and my grandfather, Elmer. After

1

Theresa died, Eleuterio would marry for a third time, to Maria Iacobucci, a cousin of Theresa's.

And yes, they also had children. But Maria had children of her own as well, from a previous marriage, and so, the family got a smidge more complicated. To the marriage, Maria brought Domenic, Dora, and Margaret. With Eleuterio, she had Francis, Christina, Eleanor (not to be confused with Eleanor-who-died, hence the clarification of –who-died.), and Maria, who passed away as a child.

In case you weren't keeping count, that's fourteen kids.

Take that, Bradys.

With fourteen kids, some of whom had no blood relation, one would probably expect that sharp divisions existed, and squabbles made up most of the interactions. But to hear any of the siblings tell stories of growing up in such a blended family, you'll hear very little of anything of the sort. There were no clarifications of half- and step-siblings. They were simply brothers and sisters, no questions asked. Perhaps this was because it was easier than explaining the links and connections, but to watch them interact, even now, when only four are left, and to hear them talk about their siblings now gone, it's obvious that the real reason was that they genuinely, honestly considered each other full siblings, that they loved each other deeply.

And most of all, they had a whole lot of fun.

Like many young men of his generation, Papa went into the Navy. For awhile he was stationed in Kansas – a source of consternation even in later years, because, of course, "there's no damn ocean in Kansas!" – and for a period of time between 1944 and 1945, found himself at the Naval base in Deland, Florida. When he came back home to Aliquippa, he eventually married my grandmother – and the story he always told about how he ended up falling for her and marrying her was debunked just last year by his sister Dora, who said that all of the "reluctance" he said he displayed was absolutely fictional – and they had four children: my aunt Christine, my uncle David, my mom, Marianne, and my uncle Michael.

My mom's generation was also incredibly close; the cousins considered each other friends first and cousins second, and the time spent with aunts, uncles, cousins, and friends was plentiful – and plenty of fun. Old photographs reveal parties the likes of which I don't think could be recreated now, and the sheer volume of family is kind of unbelievable.

But I guess that's what happens when your dad has eight living siblings, all of whom had children of their own, and your grandmother had an entire army of cousins, to boot.

Perhaps his family might have been the original Brady Bunch, but he, as an individual, was like an amalgamation of many different characters from many different media.

In his younger years, to hear him tell it, he was the quintessential leading man, a McDreamy of sorts for the 1940s and 1950s; handsome, charming, and suave – but faithful, oh so faithful and devoted. The son of a demanding father, perhaps he saw himself also as one of the Corleone boys from *The Godfather* trilogy. (Though certainly, he was no Fredo.) As a father himself, he became something of a figure straight out of a Jane Austen novel – although he was the breadwinner, the head of the household, he deferred to his wife as the *real* disciplinarian. In later years, he was Archie Bunker, blunt and maybe a little bit offensive, a man who would speak his mind without any concern about who was nearby to hear, or about whether or not he should actually say it, but absolutely endearing, and when it came down to it, fiercely protective of his children.

As a grandfather, he was Richard Gilmore; affectionate, doting, and eager to share his own loves and interests with his grandchildren. And most of all, as a friend, a brother, an uncle, he was Albus Dumbledore. Unfailingly wise, attentive, and intuitive, he would try to solve the problems of anyone who came to him, and he would be there for anyone who wanted, or needed, his attention.

And okay, maybe he saw himself as a little bit of Vito Corleone thrown in there, too. He always sort of fancied himself a Godfather, despite being distinctly unaffiliated. His domain was his family, and he knew that he was the guy in charge.

To hear him tell the stories of his childhood, of his teen years, of his days in the Navy and the shenanigans he and his buddies got up to, of the years following his return home and his courtship of my grandmother, the stories of the childhoods of my mom and her siblings, of the things he had done, the things he had seen…and okay, maybe even the things he'd just made up because they had sounded good, like the fact that he was the Elmer in question in Elmer's Glue…was a joy that many people still talk about.

Once you'd heard a story from the master of storytelling, there really wasn't any going back.

He could spin words with the best of them, conjure up pictures as vivid as anything, and he could keep an audience captive for hours upon hours. The fun factor was only magnified when he and his siblings would get together and tell joint stories, bantering and bickering about the "real" story, questioning the validity of each other's contributions to the overall tale, because when they got together and painted their pictures of what it was like to grow up as Maroccos, no one could resist listening.

And once you started listening, you never, ever wanted those stories to end.

In many ways, I think my love of words comes from him. I learned firsthand, at a very young age, the power that storytelling had. It could captivate, it could make people smile, it could transport you to another place and time, and it could immortalize one moment in time that otherwise might have seemed so simple and trivial.

Nothing about him was simple, and nothing about him was trivial. He was larger than life, a big-hearted guy full of many talents, and a whole lot of love to give to the world. He knew everyone, everyone knew him, and everyone loved him. He could make you feel like the most important person in the world, and he could make you feel like you could do anything.

He was special that way.

I hope that you enjoy these stories, and while I will never, ever profess to be even half the storyteller he was – no one ever could be – I do hope that this little book will entertain you, make you smile, and touch your heart. All of the stories might be lacking that twinkle that would have come from having them told by him - with him, it was all about listening to that big voice, full of laughter and joy as he spun a tale, and all I have here are words on a page, which will never, ever be able to capture that special spark, but it is from him that I learned how to tell a story.

And so here, and now, I happily tell you some of his.

chapter one.
if you want something, ask for it.

"Can I have that?"

This is the question that no one has ever been better at asking.

Some people ask for things because they need them, some because they want them.

And some people ask for things just because they like asking for them, or to see if they can convince someone to give them up.

And *then* there are some people who ask for things because of a reason that is some kind of amalgam of all of them, and that was Papa. He liked asking for things because he liked to have things, and he liked testing the boundaries of how many things he could ask for before someone finally told him no.

Considering that it was impossible to tell him no, boundaries were nonexistent. He could ask, and ask, and people would be more than happy to give.

First example? Whenever we would tell him that we had tickets for Pirates games, the first thing out of his mouth would be "...what are ya' gonna' get?" Meaning: "Are they giving anything away tonight?" And if the answer was something he found satisfactory and felt would be a good addition to his collection of stuff, he would grin. "Good. Bring me one." Considering we rarely needed duplicates of the giveaways, one would inevitably find its way down to his house, and would occupy a place of honor for awhile.

You know, until something else came along that he decided he liked better.

It was one of the funniest things in the world, to be perfectly honest, because there was nothing more fun than seeing his face when he successfully convinced someone to give him something. Whether it was something to play with, something to collect, or something to eat, he was excited about it. Some of my favorite stories encompass all of those categories…

***

He really liked pillows and blankets. At one point, his couch had so many throw pillows on it that you had to move them in order to have room to sit, and while he didn't mooch that particular batch from anyone – he went shopping one day, and they were on sale, so he bought a bunch. Why he needed pillows with lighthouses and flowers and teddy bears (separately, not all on one pillow!) when none of those things were really included in the décor of his living room was anyone's guess, but he wanted them, so he bought them – he loved them.

When I moved all of my stuff back home after my first year at Duquesne, we stored a lot of the bigger stuff at his house, since he had extra space that was also more readily-accessible than it would have been at our house. As I sat on his living room floor unpacking some boxes, re-sorting into stacks of 'stays at Papa's' and 'comes home,' I pulled out a soft, fleecy pink blanket.

From his spot on his couch, he eyed me, my pillow, and my blanket. "Let me see that blanket," he said, ever straightforward. I handed it over, and he promptly unfolded it, wrapped it around himself, and looked down at me again. "This is a *nice blanket*," he said, nestling in as he sent a pointed look.

"…do you want it?" I asked.

"If you're not going to be using it…"

"…you can have it."

"Thanks!"

It went very well with the soft pink pillow he weaseled out of me before I even moved my stuff into my dorm room the previous August. He slept under that blanket every night for five years, and the pink pillow was one of many that decorated the double bed in the "big bedroom," the one that had been his bedroom when Grandma was alive. In recent years, he had instead chosen to sleep in the "little room," which had a twin bed, and eventually also came to be home to his trusty little refrigerator, or on the couch downstairs. In his last few months, he had taken to sleeping on the couch, because it had become next to impossible for him to get out of the twin bed by himself. But he treasured that blanket, and that pillow, and now that both have come back into my possession, that makes them even more special.

And it makes the blanket just a little warmer.

***

In Western Pennsylvania, we're graced with the knowledge that we are responsible for some pretty great sports heroes, all across the board. While Mike Ditka may have grown up in our plan, his father served on the Board of Directors with my grandpa, and his mother is a dear friend of the family, there was one sports star who shone brighter than all the rest in Papa's eyes.

Arnold Palmer.

The golfer was the epitome of class, an athlete worthy of the gentleman's game, and Papa idolized him. (Sometimes we think he pretended he was Arnie when he was out there on the links himself, though he'd also be the first to admit that, while he wasn't too bad, he'd also never been a shoe-in for the PGA.) He watched golf religiously anyway, but when Arnie was in a tournament, you could bet that he would be glued to his television watching to see what was going to happen.

Once Arnie retired from the sport – and there may or may not have been a few very manly tears shed the day he finished his last hole at Augusta National – there were a few golfers that he kept an eye on (Phil Mickelson was one of them), but none ever earned the same kind of utter, unfailing respect that had been given to Arnie.

When Papa found out that the Pittsburgh Pirates were playing a game around Palmer's 80th birthday, were using that game as a birthday celebration for the Latrobe-born Masters champion, *and* that the game would feature a giveaway of Arnold Palmer bobbleheads, he lit up like a kid at Christmas. "Are you going to my man Arnie's birthday party?" he asked, having heard the news on the...well, on the news.

"As a matter of fact, we are," my mom replied, and I grinned, knowing exactly what was coming.

"Good. Bring me one of those bobblers." It was said so matter-of-factly, that we couldn't help but laugh. Sure, we knew that we would end up giving him one – this was his hero we were talking about, after all – but it was still funny, because *he* knew we knew we would give him one. The only problem was that, unlike most of our other Pirate giveaways, this one would be a little bit harder to split up. At the time, I was in my senior year at Duquesne, and in my dorm, there was a spot on my shelf that had been looking for something to fill it. We also have a shelf of bobbleheads in our house, and *that* shelf had a spot ready and waiting for its new addition.

Dilemma.

But, when we got to the game, we walked through the gates, and received our bobbleheads from a very pleasant PNC Park employee. Throughout the course of the game – which we ended up leaving just after the seventh inning due to increasingly cool temperatures, poor play by the Pirates, annoying people behind us, and the fact that I had an early class the next morning – we tried to figure out which bobblehead was ultimately going to move in with Papa. As we headed for the gates, we spotted the same pleasant employee, who was packing up the bobbleheads that hadn't been lucky enough to be given away. Jokingly, my mom said to him "I don't suppose we could have one of those extras; we have express orders from my dad to bring him one." He looked thoughtfully at the pile of bobblehead boxes, picked one out, inspected it, and handed it over.

"This box looks a little dented," he said with a grin, and voila! Thanks to the kindness of that man, and a little bit of jostling somewhere along the line, Papa got his very own, not-sort-of-hand-me-down, Arnold Palmer bobblehead. Arnie immediately received a spot of honor on top of Papa's entertainment center in his "music room," right next to the canvas of Bill Mazeroski leaping around the bases after hitting the home run that won the 1960 World Series, the photo of Frank Sinatra, and the Freddy Sanchez All-Star bobblehead that he got when we all went to the game for my eighteenth birthday. When he opened that bobblehead box, he smiled widely. "Looks just like him," he said. Mission: Get a Bobblehead had succeeded.

***

Our homes are set against a back hill that slopes down from some woods, and our yards are shaded by a pretty good amount of standalone trees. Therefore, we're pretty well-stocked with furry little critters who have become increasingly domestic. Namely, we have squirrels. These squirrels are as friendly as anything, and they have come, over the years, to expect that there will, at all times, be small piles of snacks set on certain porches solely for their consumption. Papa's porch was one of them. He was the first person I'd ever seen – besides the Bird Woman in *Mary Poppins* – who could get animals to sit so close to him while he tossed them food. He happily tossed dry-roasted peanuts to the bouncy animals as they cavorted around the yard, slathered peanut butter on crackers to pile on the porch, and after visits to the Texas Roadhouse, gave them the peanuts he'd loaded up on specifically for them.

During a visit that my parents and I took to see my other grandfather's sister in Sharon, Pennsylvania during the summer of 2009, we stopped at Daffin's, which has been a must-stop destination during every visit to Aunt Mary's. While my mom, Aunt Mary, and I wandered the aisles upon aisles of chocolates, hard candy, and other glorious treats, I stopped in front of a shelf that bore stuffed animals. (No, I couldn't have cared less that I was turning twenty-one in less than two months by that point. I love stuffed animals.) There was a stuffed squirrel staring me right in the face. I had to have him.

Thanks to so much time spent with Papa, I, too, had developed an affection for the needy little buggers, and had come to quite love squirrels. They're entertaining, and they're adorable. And the ones that live in our backyard have come to like me, too. They come when I call them, as they did with him, and they'll sit on the porch and contentedly crunch away on whatever we've chosen to put out for them. Feeding the squirrels was another one of our many traditions, and so when the squirrel came with us as we went down to his house to deliver the sugar-free chocolates and other candies we'd brought for him, announcing that we had something for him, his eyes lit on the squirrel, and he reached for it.

"Hey, thanks!" he said gleefully, plucking the squirrel off the couch.

I shook my head. "Well, *that's* not it, he's going to live in my dorm. We brought you candy!" I told him, handing over the bag, which was filled with everything from chocolate-covered pretzels to fruit-flavored hard tack. He looked at the bag, looked back at the squirrel, and then looked at me. Grudgingly, he handed the squirrel back, and took the bag of goodies.

"That's not fair," he said grumpily, digging in to the chocolate-covered pretzels.

It was, quite possibly, the only time in the world I'd ever not given him something when he said he wanted it. But he had candy, and chances were, he really was more excited about that than he was about a stuffed animal. The squirrel lived on my desk in my dorm room that year, and now lives in my room; it became a talisman of sorts during the World Series this year, when the now-infamous "Rally Squirrel" made its appearances during the NLCS between the Phillies and the Cardinals.

When one takes into account that Papa loved the Cardinals more than he loved any other professional baseball team — yes, possibly even more than the Pirates — and that a squirrel scrambling across the field was what marked the changing of the tides in their bid for the Fall Classic, well…

I have to wonder.

***

If you were eating something, the same rules that applied in elementary school applied with Papa. You had to have enough to share, or you couldn't have any yourself. Candy of any sort was especially part of that rule, particularly the sort of candy that comes in individual, bite-sized little pieces…like M&Ms. When Pretzel M&Ms hit the shelves, any time he saw a commercial, he'd look thoughtfully at the television screen. "I'm gonna' have to try those," he'd say, but as soon as the commercial was over, he'd forget about them.

During one of his stays in the hospital, the gift shop-slash-café downstairs happened to have them. We bought a package and headed up to his room. Sometimes, we would bring food with us to see how long it would take him to ask for it, and other times, we would just give it to him right away. (Like when we would bring him Frostys or a little bit of whatever we'd made for dinner to help him battle the mess that was tasteless, bland, and boring hospital food.) That night, it was a test night. After we'd sat there for awhile watching *SportsCenter* on the awkwardly-tilted television set mounted on the wall, I pulled out the package of M&Ms. At the first sound of a crinkling candy wrapper, his ears perked up.

"What do you have there?" he asked, and I held up the bag. He promptly, silently, and oh so pointedly stuck his hand out, palm up. He didn't need to say a word. I poured him a handful of M&Ms, and he popped them all into his mouth at one time. After a few seconds of chewing, he paused. A few more seconds of chewing, then he swallowed them.

"Hm," was his inconclusive reaction to the treat he'd been so excited on so many occasions to try.

"What's wrong? Do you like them?" I asked. He shook his head, though not in a "no, I hate them" kind of way. It was more of a surprised, disbelieving shake of the head. His mouth turned up in a small smile.

"I'll be damned. They actually have pretzels inside," he said.

Then he put his hand out again.

"More."

And, of course, it was aye, aye, Skipper.

***

Another one of the funniest food-mooching stories involves the first time Papa ever saw pita chips. I was introduced to pita chips during my freshman year at Duquesne, when ShortStop, the little convenience store, started carrying them. I quickly became addicted, and that addiction kept up for the duration of my time there. The first time he saw them was right after my senior year, when stores around my house finally began carrying the brand to which I was partial. I took a bag down to his house with me to share. Like the M&Ms story, the second he heard the tell-tale crackle of some kind of snack food wrapper, his interest was one-hundred percent piqued.

"Whatcha got?" he asked, putting his hand out for the bag.

"Pita chips."

"What?"

"Chips."

"These don't look like chips. …Open 'em up, let me have one."

We cracked open the bag – they were plain, sea-salt only – and within an hour, the bag (a supposedly party-sized one) was empty. He looked at the bag as if by staring at it hard enough, its contents would replenish themselves, then over at me. "No more? That bag wasn't very full."

"You like them?"

"Bring more of those," was his answer. And in Papa-speak, that was a ringing, glowing endorsement. I brought a few other flavors – he liked the parmesan, garlic, and herb ones (because of course he did, as you'll learn in Chapter Six), but the multigrain ones weren't quite as much of a hit – and at one point, brought hummus for dipping. That's when he realized that the pita chips were *actually* toasted pieces of pita bread. They wouldn't ever replace his love of potato chips or Chex Mix, or Goldfish, but they weren't so bad.

***

My favorite story of Papa asking for something involves my Duquesne ring. People tell me all the time that I should be so proud to have it, because it's one of the most recognizable rings in the world. (In the area, maybe, but sometimes I think 'in the world' might be a bit of a stretch.) But even if it isn't internationally-recognizable, it's still pretty distinctive. The second I told Papa what my college decision was, he was excited. Not because I'd gotten in at all, not because I'd gotten a scholarship, not because I was staying in the area (although I like to think that all of those were factors, too).

The first thing he said was "you're gonna' have one of those rings!"

I hadn't even taken my first class, and he was already thinking about the day I'd get my ring.

I got my ring as a sophomore; it arrived in the mail at home during the week, and so I didn't actually put it on my hand until the following Friday night when I got home for the weekend. It was a different shape than my high school ring, wider. It felt different, and a little bit strange on my hand. (I was also really glad that I didn't take the advice of a few people who had told me to get the biggest one. I'd gotten the small one, and it still looked huge on my hand.) But I had it.

First thing Saturday morning, I headed down to Papa's house to show him. I took it off and handed it to him for inspection, and after a very thorough study of the ring, he tried to put it on his pinky. With a disappointed frown, he looked back up at me. "It doesn't fit!" he exclaimed mournfully.

This wasn't much of a surprise, as I have very small hands and fingers, and his hands were much bigger.

"Well, no," I said, shaking my head.

"But I thought you were going to let me wear it!"

He had really been looking forward to wearing a Duquesne ring and inviting people to ask where he'd gotten it. Unfortunately, it didn't fit his pinky, and he certainly wasn't going to actually buy one that *did* fit him, so he grudgingly gave it back to me. I wore it for the rest of that year in place of my high school ring, and I eventually got a little more used to the weight and shape on my hand.

Before I moved back into school the next fall, I asked him for the chain he always wore around his neck. I unclasped it, slid my ring off my finger, and over the end of the chain. I re-clasped the chain, and handed it back to him. He looked at it, then back at me. "What's this?" he asked.

"It fits on your chain. So. You can wear it now."

Even though he had commented about the ring not fitting his hand, we both knew that he hadn't really expected me to hand it over. But I went back to wearing my high school ring – which has his signature engraved inside, where the graduate's initials would traditionally go, something for which I'm grateful every single day – and he wore my Duquesne ring on his chain. People noticed it even then, and he got to tell people about it.

He gave it back to me right before graduation, and even though he wasn't able to come to the ceremonies, having the ring and knowing he'd had it for the last year sort of made it feel like he was there. After graduation was over, and we went down to his house to show him the program and the pictures my mom had taken, I asked him if he wanted the ring back to wear again.

He said no thank you.

I wear my Duquesne ring on my right hand, a claddagh on my left for my other grandpa, and my high school ring on a chain around my neck with one of Papa's crosses, and two of his charms. And every time I look at the Duquesne ring, I have to smile.

He did.

***

13

It's become an affectionate joke now, that we see things and say "can I have that?" When we go to Pirates games on nights that promotional items are being given away, there's always a second's worth of thinking "oh, he'll be so excited to get one of these!" because it had become second-nature to hand one off.

I look at the things that he once asked for and got, and I think about the conversations that took place, and I can't help but smile. I curl up in the blanket – and the blankets that were his first, that I have now – and I hug the pillow, and I know that it's kind of like a hug. I look at the bobbleheads, and the books, and the other giveaway items, and I realize that it wasn't always about him asking for things to have them. It was him asking for things so that we knew he was interested in the things we did, and the things we liked.

And that he passed along so many of the things he loved, whether they were physical belongings, or things more like traits and habits, to me.

But really, the lesson is simple: if you want something, all you really have to do is ask for it. The worst someone can say is no. Except in his world, there was no chance of anyone ever really saying no and meaning it. So the next time you hear someone say "can I have that?" I hope you'll think about these stories.

I do.

chapter two.
always bid one dollar.

Eleven o'clock on weekday mornings might seem like a completely inconsequential time to most people. Sure, it might be lunch time for students or people out in the work force. It might be the time of your favorite class. It might be the time you go to church. It might be the time you leave for the grocery store.

For Elmer Marocco, it was a sacred time.

From eleven o'clock until noon, Monday through Friday, there was absolutely no other option for how to spend his time.

At eleven o'clock, *The Price is Right* came on.

God forbid you call him, knock on his door, or otherwise interrupt him in any way. If you wanted to talk to him in the morning, it better have been before the clock rolled over to eleven on the dot, or else you'd have to wait until the clock rolled over from eleven-fifty-nine. There was no way he was going to miss a second of his favorite game show just because someone wanted to say hello or ask him a question.

They could wait.

He scheduled doctor's appointments around *The Price is Right*, rushed home from eating breakfast after nine o'clock Mass just to make sure he was in front of his television well before the first contestant was called to "come on down!," and occasionally turned down other breakfast or lunch dates just because they would interfere. He just really liked being able to sit down in front of the television for an hour or so, and play along with the contestants.

And once, he got the chance to be in the audience. He was visiting his aunt in California, and he and some of his cousins went to the studio where *The Price is Right* is filmed, hoping to join the ranks of the lucky few hundred who would be admitted to the studio to watch an episode being filmed. And, of course, possibly to hear their name called to Contestants' Row. They were, and while none of them got the opportunity to stand behind those colored panels and bid on amazing prizes, or to go up on stage and play one of the famous games, they did *sit* right behind Contestants' Row, and so they were, technically, on *The Price is Right*.

"I was there, you know!," he liked to remind people. "I sat right there, and I could see everything. I saw my girl, she wasn't very far away. She was beautiful," he would always add.

He meant Holly, the model. She was his favorite, the epitome of beauty as far as he was concerned. (We think it had something to do with her being a redhead.) When she left the show, he was so disappointed. But not even the disappointment over being separated from Holly could compare to his sadness when the long-time, spangled-jacketed announcer Rod Roddy died. None of the announcers who took up the microphone after that could ever live up to old Rod, and Papa made sure people knew that he just *did not* like any of the new guys.

But before that first of several changes that would shake up the show as he knew it, and then despite it, his love for *The Price is Right* was unwavering. And when I was little, he would draw up a chart, sectioning it into the first set of three bidding games, the first Showcase Showdown at the Big Wheel, the second set of three bidding games, the second Showcase Showdown at the Big Wheel, and then the Showcase. We would make our bids with the contestants, filling in the squares as the game went along - and since we couldn't spin the Big Wheel ourselves, we would throw guesses out there as to what the winning amount would be for the Showcase Showdowns – and essentially, have our own record of the game on paper by the time the KDKA news at noon came on.

It's been years since the last time we did that, and I don't think I'll ever play it that way with anyone else, but the memories are fun to have. Even if I never, ever ended up winning the all-around game. A bid every once in awhile, but never the overall show.

I suppose that was to be expected, though. I was seven, eight years old. He had years' worth of watching and understanding the show to bank on. Not to mention, he was just that smart about pretty much everything, including the prices of things. (But *Wheel of Fortune,* with both the puzzles, and our tradition of trying to guess what color Vanna's dress was going to be, and *Jeopardy!*, those were competitions that were usually up for grabs.)

After Rod Roddy died, it didn't seem like there was anything that could shake up the show more. Sure, he didn't like the new guys, but he just sort of ignored them. Suddenly, the role of the announcer didn't seem so important, because he didn't think any of those guys were able to *make* it seem important. Even the revolving door of models didn't seem all that earth-shattering. But when Bob Barker announced that he was going to be hanging up his microphone and leaving the show, there was very nearly a one-man uprising.

They were going to *dare* to replace the man who was the face of *The Price is Right*?

As far as Papa was concerned, that was the worst idea in the world, and he couldn't believe that Bob was walking away. There was no one capable enough to replace him, and if they tried, then the show was doomed. He was insistent that Bob Barker leaving meant that people wouldn't watch the show, and it would be cancelled. When we pointed out that game shows got new hosts all the time, and that it hadn't necessarily doomed every single one of them – *Family Feud* was still running, and it'd had how many hosts since it first came on the air? *Jeopardy!* was still fine – he just shook his head. None of those shows were *The Price is Right*. And as far as he was concerned, *The Price is Right* would only be *The Price is Right* if Bob Barker was the one patrolling the stage.

So when the announcement came down that Drew Carey was going to be the new host, Papa announced that his show, the one he'd spent so long watching, was dead. This new guy – for he'd never really seen Drew Carey before – wasn't going to be as good, he had no idea how to host, he didn't look as suave as Bob Barker always had; the list of complaints went on and on. And, being someone who also gets extremely attached to shows (I wonder where I got that?), and who has been known to throw a few fits of her own when television casts – or baseball teams – change, I understood his pain.

But I also didn't think he was actually going to give up on it. Having been a fan for so long, he felt like it was more his show than Drew Carey's, and he wasn't going to let some new guy chase *him* away. So he kept with it – and he may have had a day of mourning when Bob's last show aired – and as time went by, to his surprise, he started warming up to Drew. No, he'd never quite replace Bob, but he wasn't so bad. Once he shook off the jitters that undoubtedly came from stepping into such iconic shoes, he slowly began to relax, to establish his own sort of hosting routine, to bring his own personality to *The Price is Right*.

And even Papa had to admit that the show had gained an air of cheerful playfulness that hadn't been there during the Barker years. The set was updated to look a little more modern, though it retained the bright color scheme, and a few new games were introduced to exist peacefully with the classics.

What Papa noticed the most though, was that suddenly, the models weren't just pretty faces whose sole purposes were standing in the background in tight dresses. They didn't all have to wear the same dress, they weren't stick-thin, and they interacted more with both Drew and the contestants. As Holly once had, there was one who stood out among the lovely women, and that was Rachael. A pretty blonde, Papa liked her smile, and the fact that she was always smiling – and not in a fake, model-esque kind of way.

That he noticed their changing role said a lot.

One morning, when Rachael came out to show the members of Contestants' Row the prize on which they would be bidding, he looked over at me, very seriously, and pointed to the screen. "Rachael got married this weekend. She married a baseball player." Not two seconds after he said that did Drew pause after the description of the prize.

"By the time this episode airs, our Rachael's going to be married. Congratulations!" he exclaimed, and the audience applauded. Rachael smiled, and laughed, and accepted the congratulations graciously. Papa looked back over at me, and shrugged.

"I told you."

Yes, yes he had.

The point is that no matter how adamant he had been that the show would just not be the same without Bob Barker, that it was bound to tank and therefore ruin his long-standing tradition of watching *The Price is Right* at eleven o'clock every single morning, he stuck with it, just because it was his show. A loyal fan, he came to accept Drew as the show's new face, and, even if he wouldn't admit it outright – at least, not if he was paying attention to what he was saying – he sort of grew to like him. As Drew started losing weight, Papa would remark on the progress with each episode. "My boy Drew's looking good," he'd say, and if my mom was around, we'd sneakily smile at each other while he wasn't looking.

Yes. Drew Carey had been accepted by the king. Not everyone got the honor of being called "my boy" or "my girl."

When he got home from the hospital in December 2010, he started having therapists and home health nurses come to the house. The physical therapist usually came in the morning, around…you guessed it, eleven o'clock.

That wasn't going to work out.

When Papa first met the physical therapist, he made it clear that even though they were working on the therapist's schedule, they were also going to have to adapt *that* schedule to *his* schedule. To his credit, the therapist was great about it, and indulged Papa. They did all of their exercises in the living room, where Papa had full view of the television; if they were going to work on standing exercises at the sink, they did them during the commercial breaks.

The home health nurse even sat and watched with him for a few minutes sometimes, playing along with him, debating whether or not that was an obnoxious amount of money to pay for something as simple as a set of dishes. He appreciated that even though they were working on a tight schedule, and that even though this was something he'd never had to do before, they were doing what they could to make sure that he felt like things were the same as they'd always been.

And they seemed pretty happy to do it. There was learning going on on both sides of the coin; he learned some exercises, and they definitely learned a thing or two about how to make good bids on *The Price is Right*.

Anyone who was lucky enough to spend time with him during the show learned a lot. They learned how to make smart bids, they learned the ins and outs of almost all the games, and they learned that, no matter what, the first prize is always worth around a thousand dollars, so bidding any higher than that is an automatic bust, and if you *do* bid more than a thousand dollars, you probably shouldn't have been picked to be in Contestants' Row.

They learned that jumping around and screaming just earns you a roll of the eyes and a disgusted frown. ("All that hootin' and hollerin', let's just get on with the game!") They learned that the Big Wheel really is heavier than it looks. They learned things about the models' personal lives, like the fact that Rachael was marrying a baseball player.

They learned that a bid of one dollar is usually a pretty safe way to go.

But the thing I think of most when I watch *The Price is Right* is of the first time Papa got his stair-lift for his house, and on his way up, began to yodel like the mountain climber in the game.

We all make sure to watch the show at least once in awhile, and one thing is for certain.

There was no bigger fan than he was.

I mean, really. He yodeled.

Yodeled.

chapter three.
that's not real music.

People who know me know that I probably wouldn't be able to name ten currently-popular music artists if my life depended on it. And even if I could name them, I probably wouldn't be able to tell you what their most famous songs are, and I *definitely* wouldn't be able to sing any of them.

It's been that way for pretty much my whole life – with the exception of the late 90's and early 2000s when everything was boy bands and every little girl could rattle off their favorite group's entire discography – and I'll tell you right now:

It's because of my grandpa.

From the time I was old enough to remember, my life was filled with the sounds of the 1940s and 1950s. Suave crooners with unparalleled charm, swingin' guys with smooth, distinctive voices, backed by some of the best Big Bands around. The most prevalent of these artists was none other than The Chairman of the Board, Ol' Blue Eyes himself, Frank Sinatra.

As far as Papa was concerned, Sinatra was the be-all, end-all of music, and there were very few people who could ever come close to reaching the same pedestal on which the good ol' boy from Hoboken had been placed.

Especially not that upstart rock-and-roll singer Bruce "Springstreet," who was another one of the very first musicians to whose work I was introduced at a young age. The Boss obviously didn't come from Papa, who had nothing but the utmost disdain for rock-and-roll, claiming that it was just a whole lot of yelling without any musical value whatsoever, but from my mom.

Neighbors commented a lot on the fact that my musical tastes were never really like the rest of the kids around. I never took it as a bad thing. It was fun to listen to music that Papa liked; the voices were good, the music was great, and it made me feel grown-up. That some of the first songs I could sing when I was little were "C'e la luna," taught by Papa, and "Sherry Darling," taught by my mom, still kind of makes me laugh. Papa and I would have sat on the back porch and sing "C'e la luna" all day if we could have…and sometimes, we did.

I knew *Italian.*

That was cool.

Of course, when I heard other versions, I got mad. They weren't singing the words as I had learned them – as Papa had taught them to me – and so clearly, they were wrong. It was offensive.

But it's just one of the many examples I have of how indelibly his musical taste, and knowledge, marked my own. Whenever I hear it now, I tap my foot, and think of how all he would have to do would be to hum the first few notes, and we would be off and singing.

He had the greatest voice, he really did. It wasn't even so much that he could carry a tune – even though he could – but more that when he sang, you could see how much he loved to, and how much he loved the songs themselves. Whether he was doing his best Sinatra impression, or warbling along with Barbra Streisand and pretending like it was a duet, he would smile the whole time, and he would add as much flair to the song as he possibly could.

He would have a blast.

***

Now that we've worked our way back to talking about Sinatra – a logical place to return when talking about Papa and music, because again, everything musical came back to Frank – it's time that we talk about the reaction he had one Friday in May, 1998.

St. Titus Church used to have fish fries every Friday during the year, without fail. With the dining area manned by the gentlemen who were members of the Holy Name Society, and the kitchen run smoothly by "the ladies," it was the church's highest-earning fundraiser, and a point of destination for people in the valley. (Beaver County might not seem all that important, but if anything can be said for it, it's that this place knows how to do food, and when Titan Hall was at its peak, there were very few churches –

if any — who could have competed with the food offered at St. Titus' fish fries, and there were definitely none who could touch their spaghetti dinners.)

Papa was the maitre'd, and so he would pick me up from school at 2:00, we would go home and either do some homework, grab a snack, or catch a bit of whatever was on television for an hour, get his apron, and head back down to the church. He would take up his position at the front of Titan Hall, ready to direct the onslaught of traffic that would start coming through the doors at pretty much exactly 3:30, and I would sit at the table right in front of his spot, with homework, a book, or blank paper and gel pens spread out in front of me. I would keep myself busy while he served as traffic cop for the hungry guests, and when my mom arrived after work at 4:30 or so, Papa would flag down a substitute, and the three of us would sit down to eat.

That night, my mom got there, we all situated ourselves at the table I'd had staked out since the beginning of the fish fry (if familiar faces came through before my mom arrived, Papa would occasionally seat other people at "our table" with me, but as a general rule, I was the sole inhabitant of the table until it was time for us to have dinner), and Papa sighed. "I should be wearing a black band on my arm."

"Why?" I asked him, as I busied myself putting away the pens that had lain scattered around my place setting.

He looked at me mournfully, and sighed again. (He was dramatic. I also learned *that* from him.) My mom instead answered.

"Frank Sinatra died today. He thinks he should be wearing a black band because of that."

"I should be! It's the end of an era!" he retorted, hands flying up in the air. (There's a reason stereotypical Italian characters in film and television flail a lot. It's because it's true.) "Ol' Frankie…man."

We listened to Sinatra CDs for several weeks straight after that. And he slowly began amassing books, magazines, newspaper clippings, and any Sinatra CDs that he hadn't already owned.

(The last time he'd had such an emotional reaction to the passing of someone not related to him was when John F. Kennedy was assassinated; we learned this when we went through his cedar chest and several boxes full of what we had thought were family photographs. But nope. They were full of JFK-related paraphernalia.)

For about a year, he was "in mourning," and there was rarely an afternoon that didn't somehow involve listening to at least one Sinatra song. Obviously, I didn't only learn to appreciate Sinatra from him. I also picked up on how to properly lament the passing of an idol.

(For that story, see Chapter Eight, "Big Fun With the Small Screen.")

***

Papa might have regarded Sinatra as the king of music (forget that hip-shaking hustler Elvis!), but if he had a queen, it was undoubtedly Barbra Streisand. There were several of her CDs that were pretty much compulsory listening in the Marocco house; *The Christmas Album* (which he occasionally questioned, if only because he wasn't entirely sure why a Jewish woman had made a Christmas album. Not because he didn't love it, because he did. In fact, the year he gave me his tiny CD player for Christmas, he also gave me a copy of that album. It was one of my very first CDs, which is only one of the many reasons it still has a special place in my heart.) and *One Voice*. I don't know why those two were the favorites. They just were.

And to be honest, most of her other albums didn't grab me the way Sinatra's did. Don't get me wrong, I think she's remarkably talented, and that she definitely has a place in the pantheon of female artists. I just couldn't sit and listen to any of her other albums for hours on end.

The one time I told him that – after falling asleep while he was listening to the boxset of one of her concerts – he looked at me, eyes wide, like I'd just told him Santa Claus didn't exist.

Luckily, we weren't really very likely to pick her for our all-day music marathons, and so the topic never really came up again.

When he got the chance to go see her live in concert was one of the most exciting opportunities of his life, even if she *had* married James Brolin. He couldn't figure that one out. But that didn't change how he felt about being able to see Barbra...live in person...*right there*...

See Chapter Ten, "Have Remote, Will Travel."

***

I remember very clearly – and don't ask me why, because this is one of those memories that you just sort of wonder why it sticks with you – being in my uncle's living room with Papa, my cousins Natalie and Nico, and my Aunt Diana when across the television screen flashed the news that John Denver had died in a plane crash. I can't remember *why* we were there, but I remember being there, and I remember Papa shaking his head sadly.

It wasn't long after that that he bought Denver's *Greatest Hits* CD. The first time I heard it, I remember asking him when "Leavin' on a Jet Plane" had been written, because, considering the unceremonious way in which the singer departed the world, it was a little bit eerie. He explained that it had been written a long time ago, but he didn't dispute that the song had definitely taken on a different sort of aura.

It became one of my favorite CDs – there was just something about Denver's voice that was really, really lovely – and so, for Christmas that year,

23

he bought me a copy. There are a couple of songs on the disc that I will always, *always* associate with Papa, but the one that sticks out the most is "For You." It was his favorite, and I know that it's because he associated it with Grandma, and their wonderful love story. The other is "Perhaps Love," and it's simply because of the line "some say love is holding on / some say, letting go." Yes, it's written as a true love song, a romantic love song, but, at its heart (no pun intended, promise), I think there's a level in the song for all kinds of love.

As I said, there's just something really soothing about Denver's voice, and something classic about the songs on that disc, especially. They cover a range of emotions, and feature a variety of tempos, and it's still just one of my favorites. Like so many other things, I'm glad that he introduced me to it, even if its origins are based in a totally random memory.

***

It was around 2003 when *Les Miserables* first came into my life. I had learned "On My Own" for my voice lessons, and I wanted to know more about the rest of the music. Sure, I had known that *Les Mis* existed, but until then, I really hadn't had much of an idea what it was about, or what the music sounded like, or even if it would be something that I liked. When I first heard "On My Own," I was hooked. I wanted to know more. When my mother and I found a DVD recording of the concert performed for the show's tenth anniversary, the cast of which featured several performers with whom we were familiar – and whom we adored – we bought it, and we watched it.

It quickly became one of my favorite musicals.

Which obviously meant that I needed to share it with Papa.

Instead of watching the entire thing, though – it was a beautiful summer day, and we had plans to go out and hang out on the porch with a boombox and reading material – I hit all of the "important" songs. He liked "I Dreamed a Dream," though he was kind of focused on how terrible Fantine's wig was, and he marched in place while sitting on the couch during "Do You Hear the People Sing?," but I was getting the feeling that overall, it wasn't one of the musicals that was going to rock his world.

Until Colm Wilkinson started singing "Bring Him Home."

If you've ever heard Wilkinson sing at all, you'll understand the arresting quality of his voice, and the tendency it has to enchant someone immediately. If you haven't, go to the internet, and look him up – I'd suggest "Bring Him Home" as your introduction to the wonderful world of Wilkinson, obviously – and I promise, you won't be sorry.

The point, however, is that hearing that song was the first time during our *Les Mis* primer afternoon that Papa was completely and fully engrossed, and when the song was over, he looked over at me.

"That old guy can *sing*," he said, his voice full of awe. "How did he *hold that note?*"

The funny part of it is that Wilkinson was probably only in his fifties at the time the Tenth Anniversary Concert was filmed in 1995. Papa was seventy-seven at the time he watched it. So, while he probably wasn't off-base in assessing that Wilkinson was on the older side *presently*, he certainly wasn't "old" by any means at the time of the performance.

"Play that again," was the next comment, and so I did. It was like he wanted to make sure there hadn't been some malfunction in the disc, and that he really had performed the song that spectacularly. From that moment, he paid attention to the rest of the show, though that attention increased whenever Wilkinson had a song, or even a snippet of one. And after that afternoon, every once in awhile, he'd say "bring that disc down. I want to hear that old guy sing that song."

I didn't have to ask which one he meant.

***

As a general rule, Papa really didn't get along with technology. He could work his CD players, he could work his televisions, and he had finally learned how to work his cell phone enough that he could call people. (Answering it, however, was a work-in-progress, and more work than progress.)

But he had absolutely no interest in learning about a computer – though he did like to look at them – or anything that looked suspiciously small to be able to do the things it claimed.

And then he met my iPod.

It was a Christmas gift from my parents during my freshman year at Duquesne, and we had a tradition of going down to his house every Christmas morning, not only to give him the majority of his Christmas gifts, but also to show him what I'd gotten. Once he was finished opening his presents[1], I showed him the iPod. He put out his hand, I handed it over, and he proceeded to inspect it closely. "What's this?"

"An iPod. It plays music."

"…no it doesn't."

"It does. Look, the headphones plug in right here, and…"

---

[1] See Chapter Four, "Count Your Presents Before They're Wrapped," for a more-in-depth description of Papa's relationship with presents.

"Where's the music come from?"

"The computer."

"The computer."

"You plug it in, and…"

"Make it play."

"It doesn't have any music on it yet."

"Bring it down tomorrow, I want to hear it."

That was his first experience with an iPod. When I took it down the next day to prove that it did, in fact, play music, I showed him how to put one of the earbuds in his ear, and I sat next to him with the other in mine. When the first notes of the song – "Promises, Promises" – started to play, a smile of wonderment came onto his face. "Well, I'll be damned," he said, shaking his head.

Shaking his head, of course, dislodged the earbud, and he scrambled after it, hurriedly replacing it. "I should get one of these."

He quickly realized that that would be silly, considering he was still warring with the various DVD players in his house, as well as his lack of desire to learn how to work a computer. Plus, he could just share mine.

And so, we often sat on the back porch, sharing the earbuds, and listening to my iPod. A couple of times during hospital stays, we broke it out and sat on his bed listening; the nurses generally got a kick out of seeing him with a sparkly pink earbud in one ear, and he would just smile at the attention.

***

Papa was the first person I ever knew who had a CD player. In one of the rooms upstairs, there was a single bed against one wall, and against the other was a small entertainment cabinet that held his record player, his Bose speakers and the receiver for his DMX Radio (a long-ago predecessor to Sirius-XM that people might not even remember), and his five-disc CD player. Before the third upstairs-room was transformed from the "Yucka Room" – the room to which all miscellaneous objects eventually found their way, including some Christmas decorations, and Grandma's sewing gear – into "my" bedroom, the "music room" was where I would stay when I slept over. He would turn the DMX Radio receiver to a light jazz station so that I could sleep. (Even then, I couldn't sleep if I didn't have some kind of sound, and music was – and still is – the ticket.)

After the Yucka Room was transformed, and the twin bed moved in there, the Music Room looked…empty. So he decided that the small cabinet just wasn't cutting it anymore, and we went shopping for a full-blown entertainment center. We finally found one that he liked, and within a few weeks, it was installed, his recliner (his most favorite piece of furniture) was moved in there, and all of the media components had a new home. In addition to the turntable and his five-disc CD player, the television and VCR also moved in, and atop the center was his collection of CDs.

It was *quite* a collection. Not surprisingly, what had to be at least half of Frank Sinatra's discography was in residence, as well as the majority of Barbra Streisand's. Also sprinkled in over the years were Tony Bennett, Sandler & Young, Connie Francis, the Original Cast Recording of *The Phantom of the Opera,* John Denver, Nat King Cole, Andrea Bocelli, the Original Broadway Cast Recording of *Camelot,* scads of Christmas music CDs, and a few of the Three Tenors' discs.

The most-played CDs lived in a black box-shaped case, one of the ones where the cases click in, and you have to press a button to release them and take them out. When I was little, I thought that was the coolest thing I'd ever seen, and I played with it every chance I got, pressing the buttons so that the cases would spring out, and then happily clicking them back into place. I think that's probably the reason some of the buttons stopped working, and you had to work a whole lot harder to get the CDs out, to be perfectly honest.

I can't even begin to count the hours we spent in that room, with him in his beloved recliner, me sprawled on the floor with a veritable fortress of pillows, blasting music that could probably be heard, not only next door, but outside, too. (Nor could I begin to count how many times we would call, and call, and get no answer, only to go down in a panic and find him in the music room, headphones on, blissfully unaware that he had nearly caused us heart attacks. He would jolt up, go "Jeeeeeeesus, what're you *doin'*?" and then look at us like we were crazy for barging into his house in search of him. "I was right here! Geez, a guy can't even listen to his music.")

When we were cleaning out his house, I took the responsibility of cleaning out the music room. I put on a couple of the CDs I'm surprised we didn't wear out, and let them play while I was sorting through the discs and records, the DVDs, and videotapes.

I kept the CDs that he treasured most, and that made up quite a section of the soundtrack of our adventures. (I even kept Sinatra's *Duets,* despite our mutual agreement that it was one of the most ill-conceived records in the world, and couldn't really be described as anything but depressing due to Sinatra's distinct lack of anything resembling a voice at that point in his life.) The records also came to live with me, because I couldn't bear to see them get shipped off to some thrift store, left to languish in a world that doesn't often appreciate a sound recording if it's not digital, or worse, just thrown away.

And you can bet that the CDs are still in that black box-case, the buttons long-non-functional, some in the same order they've always maintained.

27

As always, Frank is right in the first spot.

***

Music has always been an important part of my life; I love most types, and I love learning about new artists. I always had to have some kind of music playing when I was doing homework, and even now, I find it easier to write with my iTunes or radio going and going and going.

And okay, maybe I'm a little bit of a music snob when it comes to comparing and contrasting the music that I grew up with – Sinatra, Denver, Streisand, Springsteen, and the gang – with the music I "should" have been listening to as a kid and a teenager, and *certainly* with most of the music now (with very few exceptions), but I'm okay with that. I'd rather be able to understand the words that are being sung, and I'd rather hear actual accompaniment instead of a pounding percussion line that sounds more like someone banging on a table than anything else, and I'd rather hear the voices of those guys and dolls than a voice autotuned to within an inch of its life. I was lucky to have someone who cared about music – who also supplied me with my very first CD player, an old one of his – teaching me the ropes, and while I may never know what "popular" music is, I like to think I've got a pretty good idea of what *good* music is.

All thanks to him.

chapter four.

count your presents while they're wrapped.

No one will ever be able to convince me that kids are the people who get most excited about Christmas. So maybe kids still have the excitement that comes from believing that Santa Claus will be making trips into the homes of every child in the world to put a boatload of goodies under their trees. But Papa had kids, a sister-in-law, a nephew, and grandchildren who would do the same job as the Big Man in Red, and he didn't even have to wait until Christmas morning, since we did our present-opening on Christmas Eve, after dinner.

Well, he had to wait until Christmas morning to get *some* of his presents, but that was because the present about which we're speaking was way too big to cart around to whichever house was hosting Christmas Eve. And we're getting to the story about what that present is, but to understand why its existence came about, we have to back up a few years.

I don't remember the exact year – I'm not sure anyone would, not really – but the year isn't the important part. It could have been any year. I just know that my cousins and I were younger, and Papa was in incomparably good health. (Well, as incomparably good as a man who'd had two heart attacks, several surgeries, diabetes, and high blood pressure could be, I suppose.) But we were all sitting around in the living room of my Uncle David's house, the beautifully-wrapped presents under the tree just waiting to be opened, to have their contents ooh'ed and aah'ed over as much as their exteriors had been.

Papa just wanted to know why the adults couldn't open their presents first.

Aunt Lynn doled out the presents in rounds, making sure that all four of the grandchildren had a present at the same time, and Papa fidgeted in his chair, impatiently waiting for the moment when it would finally be his turn.

"Come on, just rip the paper!" he would grumble, folding his arms impatiently.

Sometimes, we might have purposely gone even more slowly, just to see what would happen. Once, we were pretty sure he was really close to just jumping up and helping.

When my cousins and I were finally done opening our gifts, it was the adults' turn. Unlike the kids, the adults gave gifts according to a grab-bag arrangement, and so each person had bought a gift for one other person. If they wanted to, they could buy for everyone, but it wasn't mandatory. (If gift-giving can be considered mandatory. That would sort of defeat the purpose of it being a gift, but you know what I mean. But everyone generally bought something for everyone else, even if it was just something little, like a candle, or a book, or a piece of jewelry. Or, for the men, a pair of socks, or a tie, or something.)

The first of the adults to open a present was always, always Papa, for several reasons: one, because he was the head of the family, and so it made sense for him to start things off. Two, because if he didn't get to open a present soon, we weren't so sure that he wouldn't explode from anticipation. He would tear into the paper without any regard for the carefully- and lovingly-constructed wrapping – my aunts are fabulous gift-wrappers, with pretty paper and sparkly bows and adornments – and eagerly expose whatever was inside. He was a little bit of a clotheshorse, so when the gift proved to be a new sweater – or even better, a new windbreaker or other kind of jacket-type piece – he was extra-delighted.

To be honest, we really were never sure if what he liked more was getting the presents themselves, or if it was unwrapping them that gave him the greatest pleasure. Since the two are so closely related, that might be a mystery that will never be solved. But he would excitedly start off the second round of gift-opening, and he would wait just as impatiently as he had while we kids were opening ours, for his sons, daughters, children-in-law, sister-in-law, and nephew to open their first gifts (or second, or third) so that it could be his turn again. His mantra of "come on, just rip the paper!" was repeated over and over with every gift, and when it got around to being Uncle David's turn to open a gift, he would look pointedly at Papa, and peel the tape away as slowly as possible, fold back the paper with painstaking precision, neatness, and care, until Papa finally just let out strangled cries of "DAVID. COME ON." Uncle David was easily the best at stoking the fire of Papa's impatience when it came to gift-opening, and it was never not a source of entertainment on Christmas Eve.

Once the gifts were all open, Papa would survey the room, and the piles near each person. "What a haul," he'd always say – or at least, some variation – as he silently observed. Anyone who would have looked at him during one of those moments on any given Christmas Eve might have seen a man who was thinking about how lucky he was to be surrounded by a happy family, a family lucky enough to be able to exchange gifts in addition to being able to spend time all together for the holiday. And I'm sure that that was part of what was going on in his brain.

The other part?

The other part was counting.

One Christmas, he finished looking around the room, and his gaze had lingered just a little bit longer on his nephew Ron's pile of presents than it had on anyone else's. Throughout the evening, as gifts had been doled out, Papa had crowed several times that Ron had *just* opened a present, why was Ron opening *all* the presents, where was one of *his* presents? We all laughed, and we just kept on watching people open things. Papa eventually got to open all of his presents, so he was content.

Until he realized that his pile of goodies wasn't *quite* the same size as Ron's. "Hey. Why does he have more presents than I do?"

(I don't think Ron actually had *more* presents, because we all had one gift from each other branch of the family. So technically, everyone had received the same amount of presents, just in different combinations. Maybe one gift was a sweater, which took up a whole box, and maybe another was a big box with a couple of smaller boxes inside, but it still only technically counted as one gift. I'm pretty sure that that was the case in this particular situation. But the story's still hilarious. Perhaps funnier if you were there, or if you can imagine hearing Papa saying it, but funny nonetheless.)

No number of assurances could convince Papa that Ron didn't actually have more presents, he had just gotten more that were individually wrapped instead of all being in one box or bag, and he folded his arms across his chest and shook his head, as if he was berating everyone in the room for letting such an atrocity happen. He never let Ron live that down, saying every year after that, "Alright, let's just give Ron all the presents and go home!"

I do need to clarify that it was all (mostly) a joke, and that he wasn't really mad, per se. He just liked causing mischief, and, as we've established, he really did just like to open presents. He wouldn't have been upset if there hadn't been anything, he didn't *need* anything, and he'd be the first to tell you that. (But also, as we saw in Chapter One, "Can I Have That?" he'd also be the first to tell you if there was something he wanted. He didn't *need* it, necessarily, but if you maybe wanted to give it to him, he wasn't going to say no.)

It just became a running joke that there had been a year when Ron had gotten more presents than Papa, and so, a few years after that, my mother had the idea to buy one of those giant stockings, and to fill it with random knick-knacks, practical stocking-stuffers types of things, some books, some CDs, and other little things — all of which had been individually wrapped, of course — and to give it to him for Christmas, in addition to the "real" gifts we always got him.

That year, we took the stocking to my Uncle Michael's house on Christmas Eve (sometimes we switch up the location, just so one family isn't stuck with all the preparation every single year), and we hid it behind the couch so that he couldn't see it. After what he thought was the last gift had been opened, he sat back, and began his traditional scan of the room. "Hang on," my mom said as she stood up. "I think there's one more that we missed." She dragged the stocking out, and his eyes lit up. Somehow, he knew — or he was just *hoping* — that the giant red sock was for him, and he beamed when she put it in front of him.

When he realized that everything was individually-wrapped — thereby securing him that year's spot for "Person With the Most Presents to Unwrap" — he just kept on grinning, and said that he would open everything inside the next morning, because it would take too long to unwrap them that night; we had church to get to.

The next morning, we headed down to his house, same as always, and he looked like...well, like a kid on Christmas. He was on the edge of the couch, the stocking propped alongside him, ready to start opening away. The second we sat down after grabbing a garbage bag to gather the paper that would soon be shredded, he went for it. The stocking had things like bags of different kinds of sugar-free candy (so he could indulge his sweet tooth in a way that wouldn't directly contradict his doctor's orders), a few packages of large-print playing cards, a few CDs, a few DVDs, batteries, cleaning cloths for his eyeglasses, a pocket-sized flashlight, a small umbrella to keep in the car, handkerchiefs...really, just things that weren't really all that special, but that were good gifts in that they were completely practical.

And with every one that he opened, he looked like he had just received the best gift in the world. Each one was more exciting than the last; the playing cards might as well have been boxes full of eternally-paid-off American Express cards, and each bag of dollar-store sugar-free candy could have been mistaken for the finest chocolate Switzerland had to offer. When he finally got to the bottom of the stocking — it took awhile, it was a big stocking! — he smiled happily, looked around at the piles of little things, and promptly opened one of the bags of candy. He silently shook out three York Peppermint Patties, and he handed one to me, one to my mom, and kept one for himself.

"This was the best Christmas present," he said, and we ate our candy. (It was entirely irrelevant that it was nine o'clock on Christmas morning. Candy was absolutely a perfectly-good breakfast.)

When the next year rolled around, around the time Christmas shopping would begin in earnest, we were hanging out with him at his house. While watching *Jeopardy!*, and working at the day's crossword puzzle, without picking up his head, he said simply "that stocking's upstairs on the cedar chest, if you want it."

Subtle as a trainwreck.

My mom looked at me and laughed, shaking her head. "What makes you think you're getting it filled again?" she asked him, and his head popped up. He looked at her, eyes wide behind his reading glasses.

"No sock this year?" he asked.

She laughed again. "Run up and get it," she told me.

With something that looked suspiciously like a sigh of relief, he returned to his crossword puzzle. And for the next four years, every year, he got a giant stocking filled with miscellaneous, individually-wrapped items. He was never not going to open the most presents again. When the original stocking had to be retired – its seams had blown out, plus, it disappeared – we replaced it with a new one, and wrote his name along the top in glittery puff paint. We found the "new" stocking – whose seams were also beginning to burst – in the cedar chest when we cleaned out his house, and it, along with his Christmas tree, became part of this year's Christmas decorations at our house.

***

Just to make sure that no one takes away from this chapter that Papa was completely materialistic and some kind of hoarder or something – because he definitely wasn't materialistic...though he may have had some hoarding tendencies, especially when it came to newspaper clippings, those cards you get at funeral homes when you go to viewings, and blankets and pillows – I think there needs to be a little bit of storytelling as far as how much he liked to buy presents for people, too.

For birthdays, for special celebrations like graduations or First Holy Communions, for occasions that weren't anything at all, but "just because," he loved picking things out to give to people – though he also enlisted other people to do the wrapping for him, he was never really satisfied with the results when he tackled wrapping – and it didn't matter who you were. My mom and her two best friends go to lunch to celebrate birthdays (and every

Wednesday), and have for years. Papa also had a standing invitation, and when he knew that the gathering was going to be for a birthday and not just another Wednesday, he was always sure to bring along a little gift, usually a candle or a pretty little statue from the Hallmark store. He was always so proud of the presents he picked out, making sure that people knew he picked them out all by himself.

Then, every Christmas, he would go to the jewelry store, and pick out earrings for the women and girls in the family. Christmas 2009 – the last Christmas he was able to really get into the spirit of the holiday – I went down to his house during break, as always, and we were sitting in the living room when he said "let's go shopping." He got his cane – a fancy shillelagh-style walking stick that my uncle brought back from Ireland for him years ago – and a box of rolled quarters that he'd been squirreling away over the course of the year, bundled up in his scarf, coat, and walking cap, pulled his gloves on, and we made our way to the car.

The snow wasn't anything outrageous; it was just enough to make everything look pretty. But it sure was cold. Our first stop was at the bank, to cash in the quarters for bills, and then, we headed for the jewelry store. He bought the earrings from the same jeweler every year, so the second he walked through the door, they knew who he was, and what he was there for. Over the next hour, he studied pairs of earrings, doing his best to pick out pairs that were all equally beautiful, but individual enough to match the personalities of my aunts and my mom. When he was finally satisfied with his selections, the exchange of money and earrings took place, and they offered to wrap the earrings in store. So while the store's owner brought out a chair for Papa to sit, along with a bottle of cold water to drink, I sat with the owner's mother and labeled the small boxes with the appropriate names as soon as they were wrapped, so as to avoid any confusion at a later date.

Namely, Christmas.

He was really proud of all of the selections he'd made, and it has to be said that he had absolutely impeccable taste when it came to jewelry. That Christmas Eve, he stood up from his chair, gestured for me to get the bag he'd instructed me to hide among the other presents under the tree, and cleared his throat. "Hold on, we're not done. Santa and his elf have a few more." I handed him box after box, and he delivered them to their new owners.

Most of the earrings I own came from him, whether they were for my birthday, or for Christmas. The earrings I always wear – that I rarely take out – were from him. He gave me my pearls a week before my senior Prom, even though he'd bought them for my graduation. I wore them to Prom, to graduation, and for pretty much every occasion since then that's called for them. ("You have to wear them a lot so they stay shiny," he instructed me solemnly when he first gave them to me.)

Presents were a very important thing to Elmer David Marocco. And yes, he really did count them, and he would look absolutely indignant if he felt as though he had been slighted, or cheated, if the number of presents wasn't up to par. Granted, he wasn't ever *really* mad, but after a point, it was tradition that he grumble, and he had a reputation to uphold.

But for as much as he liked to receive them, he also liked to give them, and he was wonderful about making sure that all of the presents he gave actually meant something special. Even though he gave me several beautiful pairs of earrings, and my pearls, some jewelry that used to be my grandmother's, and a small statue of an angel that sits on the shelf in my bedroom, I think some of the best gifts he ever gave me (in addition to his love and, you know, everything I ever learned from him) were some pictures of him when he was in the Navy, and a grey T-shirt, years and years ago, with an appliquéd and sort of puffy Elmo on the front.

I think you'll be able to figure out that significance.

chapter five.

whistle while you do everything.

When it's time to come inside after a long day playing outside, or to come in for dinner, or to come home for anything else, most kids respond to their name being called.

I answered to a whistle.

No, not like the Von Trapp children in *The Sound of Music*. It wasn't that kind of whistle.

This was a whistle that was whistled by a person, a whistle that sort of defined my childhood. Whether it was a whistle he created himself, or a birdcall that he had learned how to mimic, the fact of the matter was that it was a very specific whistle. And when I heard that whistle, I answered.

Because it was *my* whistle.

I don't even know if I would be able to describe what it sounded like, to be perfectly honest, but it was a whistle that was unmistakable. When I heard it, I knew he was looking for me. And no matter where I was, I could hear it. (As long as I was where I was supposed to be. If I wasn't, and if I couldn't hear it, he would instead employ one loud bellow of my name, and then I was going to be in a whole lot of trouble once I finally answered.)

The neighbors came to recognize the whistle as his call for me, too, and if they heard it, then saw me scuttling past their doors and towards Papa's house, they'd comment. It was one of the nice things about growing up on

Linmar at that time – the neighbors actually interacted. That's not really something that can be said anymore, except to say if there's some kind of drama going on, someone will know about it because the gossip mill is alive and well, but real involvement in neighbors' lives, knowing them well, that's not the case.

And that's kind of sad.

The neighborhood now *definitely* wouldn't recognize a whistle as being a specific call for a specific person.

The teachers at Bible School one summer certainly didn't recognize it.

During the summers between the ages of about six and ten, St. Titus held Vacation Bible School every morning for a week in mid-June, sometimes mid-July depending on the availability of teachers, and whether or not the coordinators had heard a lot of feedback regarding preference for one time over the other.

It was the summer between first and second grade – which meant that it was the summer Grandma had died – because my Bible School classroom was in the annex of the school, and that was the most familiar part of the school to me at the time. I had just finished first grade, and the second grade classroom was just two doors down. The office was at the end of the hallway.

It was a nice little corner of the world.

It was also a corner of the world where I never expected to hear my whistle. Why would someone be whistling my whistle when I wasn't at home, and I wasn't supposed to be anywhere but where I was?

Until I realized that no one at Bible School would know that whistle anyway, so there was only one explanation for the whistle, and only one person could be responsible for doing the whistling. So, I looked at the teacher, looked at the door, and did the only sensible thing.

I left my project of the day on my desk, and I went in search of the source of the whistle.

I was no sooner in the hallway of the annex when Papa came out of the office, and I ran up to him, threw my arms around him, and gave him a hug. I wasn't sure what he was doing there so early – it wasn't time to go home yet! – but that was okay. It just meant that I got an extra Papa-hug for the day, and that was fine by me.

The teacher didn't seem to share my opinion that hearing my whistle was obviously an important reason – and a legitimate excuse – for leaving the room in the middle of a project and without permission, and she came out into the hallway, and looked at me. After (I presume, I can't remember what she said specifically, I just remember the look on her face) telling me that I had to come back in and stay in the classroom until it *was* time to go home, I sighed, left Papa in the office, and went back into the classroom.

Everything I Know

Knowing that he was waiting for me, and waiting to start our adventures – because every day was an adventure, and now, being his sidekick was more important than ever since he was all by himself – made the clock go even more slowly, and when it was finally time to go home, it felt like days had passed. This time, Papa came to the door of the classroom, apologized that he had caused me to leave the room, and explained that the whistle was one of our forms of communication, and the teacher just smiled.

All was well.

Really, though, he called me. I had to answer.

***

Sometimes, I would hear a birdcall that sounded *sort of* like my whistle, but I could always tell when it was a bird, and when it was Papa. When it was a birdcall, it was just loud enough to pick up on. When it was Papa, it was loud and clear, and carried easily down the sidewalk. Living only nine doors down from him meant that when we were both on our back porches, we could not only see each other, but we could have conversations if we had to.

And okay, maybe they were really loud conversations that the entire neighborhood could have heard, and that consisted of "Come down here!" and "Coming!," but they were conversations nonetheless. So, suffice it to say, the neighbors knew our dynamic, they were amused by our dynamic, and as I mentioned, they knew that the sound of a specific whistle meant my presence was being required.

As I got older, the whistle sort of fell out of use. It wasn't like I was playing outside anymore – there were no kids on Linmar anymore, and if I was outside, I was out there with him, and if I wasn't, then he just called on the telephone. It wasn't nearly as much fun as being summoned by a whistle – even if other people knew what the whistle meant, it was still something special, because it wasn't meant for anyone else – but that was okay. It was still a patch in the quilt of our adventures. And just because I hadn't heard my whistle in a really, really long time didn't mean that I'd forgotten about it.

How *could* I have forgotten it?

Apparently - to paraphrase a line from *Titanic*, which Papa and I went to see together when it came out in theaters – it isn't something that now lives only in my memory. My mom and I were at the hair salon, waiting to get our hair cut, and our hairdresser used to be Papa's next-door neighbor. Her husband was also in the shop; he'd stopped in to have his hair cut right before our appointments. My mom and Luis and Denise were idly chatting while Denise washed Luis' hair. I had a book with me, and I was sort of reading it, when I heard my whistle.

Luis had remembered it.

They hadn't lived on Linmar for years, but they had been there during the height of the use of the whistle. My head snapped up from the book, and I turned back around. I couldn't help but smile, and my mom shook her head.

"I can't believe you remember that," she said, her voice filled with wonder. Denise, too, knew the significance of that whistle, and she gave a smile of her own.

Hearing that whistle again, even if it wasn't Papa doing it, was something really special. It's been tough, not to have him around, and not to be able to share things with him, or to just trot down the sidewalk and show up at his door. I can't even say how many times I've caught myself looking down the back sidewalk, expecting him to be there on his porch, ready to put his arm in the air and wave me down.

There are some days that are worse than others, and some that aren't so bad because I stumble across little things that make me think of him in all the best ways. Hearing that whistle that day made a day that might otherwise have been forgettable one that was pretty special. As hokey and as sentimental and as whatever as it probably sounds, I think there was definitely a reason that Luis was there that day, of all the times he could have been there – heck, he probably didn't even need to come in, he could have had his hair cut at home or something – and to even think to whistle.

Especially because I have never, *ever* heard anyone, or anything, recreate that whistle perfectly. Ever.

If I wasn't already pretty sure that Papa's still sticking close to me, then that would have sealed it as a certainty.

***

He was also the one who taught me how to whistle at all; while I was never able to whistle quite like he did – even I can't mimic our whistle – he was patient while teaching me, and the first time I managed to make a sound, I think he may have been more excited about it than I was. I was just so surprised that sound had actually come out that I didn't even think to be excited about it. But his excitement was infectious, and as it dawned on me that I had actually whistled – even if it had been the tiniest of sounds, it had been a sound! – and that I'd made him proud, no matter how trivial the accomplishment might have been, I got excited. If I could finally make a sound, how soon would it be that I could whistle like he could? He could whistle anything, even full songs, and they were recognizable.

He would whistle while he sat at the kitchen table, reading the newspaper in the mornings. He would whistle while he walked to and from the car. He would whistle while he moved around the kitchen during the process of making dinner. He would whistle while he sat on the couch. And yes, he whistled while he worked. It isn't just him whistling that sticks in my mind as a very prominent memory. I also link the sound of a train whistle to him — as a former railroad man, and a proud one at that, any time we would be driving near train tracks, and the train's whistle would sound, he would put his hand to his heart, and tilt his head back and to the side like he was in an old Western movie and had been shot with an "Injun's" arrow. He'd let out a "pained" sigh, and shake his head.

So really, whistling is just one of those things that, on so many levels, makes me think of him. I'm still a disaster at maintaining a good whistle — unless it's the shrieking, piercing version my mom taught me, one I've used often — and I know that somewhere, he's shaking his head at that. He'd tried so hard to teach me how to be a really good whistler.

It must have been the token thing I just *didn't* learn.

chapter six.
there's not enough garlic.

In addition to storytelling, getting what he asked for, *The Price is Right*, and music, there's one more thing that was absolutely essential to Papa.

That was food.

I know, I know, food is essential to everyone, everyone has to eat, and so on and so forth. And food was essential to him in that way, the same way that it is to everyone else, but it was also essential to him in a different way.

He just really, really loved food. He loved to cook, he loved to watch cooking shows, he loved to have other people cook things and send them to him so he could enjoy them, and he liked to go grocery shopping.

Okay, maybe the love of grocery shopping – at least in later years – was because he liked to drive the motorized carts through the aisles and run – literally – into people he knew. ("He thinks he's Mario Andretti," was a text-message response from my mother at one point when I texted her to let her know where we were in case she tried to call the house and didn't get an answer. We've already sort of addressed the not-answering-the-phone drama. All that's really necessary to know is that sometimes, he would be incommunicado – usually because his phone had somehow been knocked off the hook without his realizing it – and it was stressful.)

But the point is, food was one of his favorite things, and not just because it was necessary. He didn't believe in eating because you had to, he believed in eating because you loved to, and he believed in eating things you loved.

And boy, oh boy, did he believe in garlic.

In his kitchen, there was no such thing as too much garlic. In everything he made – everything that called for savory flavor, that is, it wasn't like he was just putting garlic in things for the sake of having garlic in them – there was some hint of the pungent staple. Whether it was garlic powder, garlic-flavored vinegar on salads, or several cloves of the "real stuff," if you asked him to make something, you were going to get it, but you could count on getting an Elmer-ized version, chock-full of garlicky goodness. Although sometimes, it was a little…strong…for the consumption of the general public, he'd just shake his head if any complaints arose. "It's good for you," he would say, and he would happily dig in, or he'd wrinkle up his face, give you a Look, and shake his head. "Got to keep the vampires away," he once intoned, serious as anything.

The fact of the matter was that if he was making something, he was putting as much garlic in as he wanted, and if you thought it was too strong, well then, you were just going to miss out on partaking of his culinary genius.

He had no qualms about telling people when their garlic-level fell short of his expectations, either. Pork roasts, especially, were often the victims of his scrutiny, despite the fact that they had been liberally plugged with entire cloves. If you couldn't smell the garlic all around Linmar, then you just hadn't done it right, and he would shake his head with disappointment.

It wasn't just family members he would scold for being stingy with their garlic usage, either. He had no problem telling waiters and waitresses at Italian restaurants that they should tell the cook to use more garlic in the future. It just wasn't right if there wasn't enough garlic. (As you might be able to guess, there were very few Italian restaurants that earned his patronage. The only one he was ever consistently pleased by was Mario's in Beaver because of their incredible pizza, and the fact that their sauce was tart, not sweet. Nothing irritated him more – besides insufficient use of garlic, of course – than sweet tomato sauce, either on pasta or pizza.)

Of course, he was pretty partial to the sauce he made. It was a variation on my grandmother's recipe – though he insisted there was something she had done that she'd never told him, so his never quite tasted right, although it was good – but he also liked my Aunt Michele's. (When she sent him containers after she made it, there was nothing that delighted him more than being able to pull one of them out of the freezer and have pasta for dinner.)

While my grandmother was known for her sauce, among many, many other things, there were quite a few things that fell into Papa's realm of responsibility.

For Christmas Eve, it was the baccala.

Our Christmas Eve dinners followed the Italian tradition of having no meat; ours was in line with the celebration of the Feast of the Seven Fishes. We had smelts, we had linguine with clam sauce, we had shrimp, we had crab, we had tuna salad, we had one fish that changed every year – sometimes it was flounder, other times it was lobster, and sometimes it was orange roughy – and we had the baccala. Baccala is salted cod, and one must soak it thoroughly before preparing it in order to rehydrate it, and to remove the boatloads of salt that were used to preserve it without need for refrigeration. Some people might use a different time frame, but he liked to soak it for at least three days.

The baccala was his domain; he didn't tell anyone precisely how he prepared it, because he didn't want anyone to be able to replicate his secret methods. (He liked that it was *his* job, and he didn't particularly want anyone to decide that they were going to make it their job instead, to try and lighten the load on his shoulders as the years went along.) One of my most vivid sense-memories of Christmas Eve is walking into his house, and having the house smell like the baking baccala. Not in a terribly overpowering fishy sort of way, either, which was quite a feat in his small apartment. Just enough of a seafood smell that you knew it was seafood, with overtones of garlic (of course). Christmas 2010, he taught me how to prepare it "the right way," because he just didn't have the stamina to be on his feet or to haul the tray around from the table to the oven to the counter. So he supervised while I did the legwork, and it turned out pretty well.

There still seemed to be something missing – he was the one who had the magic touch - but it was close enough. For Christmas 2011, it was my job to make the baccala, and I still maintain that it wasn't perfect. But it looked right enough, and it smelled right enough, that it was *almost* like he was responsible for it. Though in a way, I suppose he was; it was his instruction I relied on, and his recipe that I followed.

But really. He was a food ninja. No matter how closely you watched him while he was putting a dish together, you could try to replicate it later, and there would just be *something* missing. The best example of his food ninja skills was undoubtedly his salad dressing. Somehow, he could pour plain old canola oil and regular red wine vinegar onto a salad, and it would be insanely delicious.

.   But when it wasn't Christmas, and baccala wasn't needed, the go-to food was roasted red peppers. He didn't roast them himself, he used Mancini's whole peppers from a jar, but what made them special was all in the preparation. I had always insisted that peppers were gross, I didn't like them – and I still don't like green ones, don't even bring them near me – but when I dared to taste Papa's red peppers (after receiving countless reassurances that no, they weren't hot), I was a believer. Red peppers really *did* taste different than green ones, and they were *sweet*. The preparation is simple, the ingredients are completely straightforward, and while Mancini's peppers do taste best, it's sometimes fun to roast your own.

But when I do them now for family things, I always use Mancini's. It's the way he would have expected me to do it.

***

I could talk about all of the other things he liked to make – soup, green beans, eggs with peppers and onions, hamburgers, chicken wings and potatoes, and French toast, to name a few – or all of the other things he liked to eat – macaroni and cheese, baked fish, omelets, and all of the things that he liked to make, of course – but there was another aspect of food that mattered: he liked to go out to restaurants to eat, and while there were very few Italian places that ever made the grade (or at least, made the grade consistently), there were four restaurants you could count on him frequenting: Cosmo's (later called Anna's) in Hopewell, the Texas Roadhouse in Center, the Lebanese Club in Aliquippa, and Taiwan 101, also in Center.

Cosmo's/Anna's, which is in the Hopewell Shopping Center, is conveniently just around the corner from Our Lady of Fatima Church, and therefore made the perfect spot for post-church breakfasting. For a few years, it was a big to-do, with a bunch of his church-friends gathering after Mass, but as time went on and members of the group moved away for warmer climates, it dwindled down. During the summer, I would go with him to church, and then I'd be his breakfast partner.

The funniest thing about Cosmo's was that it was also the breakfast place of choice for my other grandpa, Joe O'Neill. After my Grandma Betty died in 2005, Pap would continue to go to Cosmo's – by that point, I believe, called Anna's -, and sit in the same booth he'd always occupied. Sometimes my uncle would be with him, but most of the time, it was him, his cigarettes, and his plate of sausage, scrambled eggs, and "Murphys" (home-fried potatoes). Across the aisle sat Papa in *his* typical booth - without the cigarettes, and with a different choice of breakfast, but the two of them would chat (read: yell, as both were somewhat hard of hearing) across the room.

The first time I went to Cosmo's, it was with Pap, Grandma, and my cousin Stacy, because I stayed with them on Tuesdays during the summer when Papa was golfing with the guys from St. Titus. And so, I was introduced to the waitressing staff as their granddaughter (obviously). When I also started coming in on days that weren't Tuesday, and with Papa, the waitressing staff was a little bit confused...until they found out that he was *also* my grandpa. The fact that my grandpas had gotten to be buddies was something most people found pretty endearing, and I'm glad that the two of them got to have breakfast together so often; it made me feel better that both of them had a buddy, and that while they sat at different tables, they weren't lonely.

In addition to being the go-to spot for breakfast, Anna's was also a Friday night tradition. Their fish dinners were Papa's favorite – surpassing perhaps even St. Titus' – because not only did they come with enough fish to eat there, there would always be some left over to take home for the next day. *And* they came with the salad bar; considering the Friday soup was clam chowder, he was…

…well, as happy as a clam.

Now both of their tables are empty, but the fun memories of good company and good food can still be felt.

***

Anna's has a homey atmosphere about it; it's not very big, it's certainly not very loud, and the menu is just diverse enough. When compared with another one of his favorite restaurants, the Texas Roadhouse, it's a little bit funny. Every couple of weeks, it seemed, Papa was hungry for "some good ribs." Well, considering this is Beaver County, and not the heart of Texas, barbecue isn't exactly on every corner. Luckily for him and his occasional hankering, we do have a Texas Roadhouse, and for whatever reason, the loud, peanut-shell-covered, country-music-blaring restaurant was a frequent destination.

We think it may have had something to do, not only with the really good ribs, but with the fact that the peanuts were all-you-can-eat, and he could stock up for the squirrels at home. Add in the delicious rolls that came to the table with you as you sat down, and maybe the allure wasn't so hard to spot after all. The funny thing was that he never actually referred to it by name; all he had to say was "I want ribs," or "let's go to the place with the peanuts," and we would know what he meant. At one point, I think we may have made one trip a week for about a month and a half.

True, taking him to a place where he could eat extremely messy food probably wasn't the greatest idea in the world; most of the time it seemed like all he had to do was just *look* at food, and some kind of spot would end up on his shirt, or on his pants, and he would inevitably look down at it in utter dismay that yet another white shirt had been ruined by something that probably wasn't going to come out.

We used up at least two Tide-to-Go sticks on sojourns to the Texas Roadhouse. But the shirts were generally goners anyway, and when it came down to it, it didn't matter. He still wore the shirts, could probably tell you when and where the spots happened, and it definitely didn't stop him from proclaiming that he wanted ribs.

Everything I Know

Or that he wanted to watch the line-dancing waitresses.

***

Despite being fairly regular patrons at the Texas Roadhouse, in a restaurant of that size, and with such a turnover rate of staff, whether it was just by section or by actual employment, it wasn't likely that the waiters and waitresses would remember us. But in smaller restaurants, places that aren't part of a chain, and places that are just a little bit closer to home, he was definitely recognized, definitely remembered, and definitely loved. The Lebanon Mirdites' League has their local club not far from our house, and in addition to their bar, they have a small dining room at the back, and a kitchen that's open on Fridays, Saturdays, and Sundays. Non-members are welcome to come in and eat wonderful home-made lamb, grape leaves, kibbee, and hummus, plus spinach pies, rice, and salad. The menu is limited, and the dining room very small, but the fact of the matter is that the menu doesn't *need* to be huge. What they do, they do *very well*, and you don't need anything other than that.

Many of the women who run the kitchen are members of St. Titus Church, and so they were at least familiar with our family anyway. But when we started going to "the Club" pretty much every Saturday night, meeting my uncle, aunt, and cousin after church, that familiarity bloomed into friendship, into effusive greetings and hugs when we came through the door. No one received bigger, more excited hugs than Papa.

What can I say? He kind of had a fan club.

The ladies would flock to him, fussing over him as they took his order, and he loved every second of it. He loved Lebanese food, and would eat some of everything. Salad, rice, lamb, grape leaves, kibbee – though what he really wanted were the banana peppers that came with it – and pita bread…he couldn't have been happier when those things were placed in front of him. During the summer of 2010, my cousin and I planned a surprise for him; she was home from school for the summer, and my mom was away at a wedding in South Carolina, so my aunt and I were hanging out with Papa. Natalie and I arranged for her to come down, and the two of us went to pick up food from the Club. We brought it back to his house, where my aunt had been evading questions about what was for dinner for the better part of an hour or so.

When we came through the door with the food, he was delighted, and he proceeded to gobble it up like he hadn't eaten in days. Which of course wasn't true, because he had, but you wouldn't have known that if you'd seen the way he was digging in. And the fact that he was so excited about the food – which was exceptionally good -, and the company, made for a really wonderful evening.

The ladies from the Lebanese Club all came to the viewing at the funeral home. Seeing their faces in line prompted us to decide that the Saturday after his funeral – the funeral was on a Thursday – we would meet at the Lebanese Club for dinner. His sisters came, his brother came, their children came; my mom and her brothers and her sister were there, and their spouses and kids were there. We took up a fairly good portion of the dining room, so there was a definite Marocco presence. The only one physically missing was him, but even then, we all knew he was there.

There was no way he would ever have let us go without him.

***

Obviously, we weren't exactly strangers to restaurants. But our longest restaurant-relationship was with the people who were the owners, first of the Empire Palace Chinese restaurant in Hopewell, and now Taiwan 101 in Center. After Ana and her family sold the Empire Palace and moved away, we still continued to go there, but the quality of the food was definitely different. A few years ago, after Mass, we, and friends of ours, decided to give Taiwan 101, the new restaurant in the Wal*Mart plaza in Center, a try.

Imagine our surprise when we walked through the door, and there was Ana. Immediate recognition dawned all around, and the first thing she asked was "how is Grandpa?" He wasn't with us at the time, having chosen not to go to Saturday night Mass in favor of going to the 8 AM Holy Name Society Mass on Sunday (probably), but we knew immediately that we were going to need to make another trip to Taiwan 101 very, very soon.

He *loved* Ana. He was going to be so excited when he found out that not only was she back, she was back in the restaurant business.

The food was fabulous – not that that was a surprise in the slightest – and we knew then that we would definitely be rekindling an old food relationship. A few days later, my mom got home from work, and we asked him if he wanted to go get Chinese food for dinner. He replied that of course he did, and we were on our way. When it became clear that we weren't heading for Hopewell, he demanded to know what kind of Chinese food we were getting. We just told him that we had tried a new place, and it was pretty good.

When we walked through the door, he spotted her right away. He clapped his hands merrily and gave her a big hug. Needless to say, he wasn't so disappointed that we weren't going to the Empire Palace anymore. When the wait staff also proved to be a cast of familiar faces, he was sold. It was his new favorite place, and any time he was craving Chinese, out to Center we headed.

After one of the times he was released from the hospital, we were no sooner out of his room than he said "Okay, let's go eat. I'm starving."

"Okay, Dad, what do you want?" my mom asked him.

"Calamari. Let's go see my girl."

Believe it. Taiwan 101 does fried calamari better than even some Italian restaurants I've been to. It's bursting with flavor, and doesn't have the rubbery texture or overly-fishy smell that some might expect. It's flawless. And after having been subjected to hospital food, he wanted something with *garlic*.

(You're shocked, aren't you?)

Taiwan 101 might just have been his overall favorite food destination, not only for the food itself, or for the "fancy" paper napkins that he liked to hoard, but for the atmosphere of friendship that existed. He loved Ana, and he thought very highly of her sons, her husband, and the wait staff. He was grateful that they were always so welcoming to us, and to him, when we came through the door, and that she remembered him as fondly as he remembered her.

The first time I went to the restaurant after he died, Ana asked me on my way out how he was doing. Telling her that he was gone was *so* hard. Her eyes teared up, and she shook her head. "I'm going to miss him," she said simply, and she gave me a hug.

If that isn't the sign of a wonderful person, who truly appreciates her customers, I don't know what is. But I can say one thing for certain; he'd have appreciated that. A lot. What was more, the time after *that*, the rest of the wait staff made it a point to tell us how sorry they were to hear, and that they would all miss him.

When we were cleaning out his house, I reached into the pocket of a jacket, and in it, I found a folded-up napkin, one of the ones he liked so much, from Taiwan 101. I realized that the last place he had actually gone out to eat was there. And now, whenever we go, and look at those napkins, I hear a little whisper:

"Keep that napkin. I like those."

***

There was also a period of time where shows about food were almost as important as food itself. We graduated from *Epicurious* and *Great Chefs of the World* to the more specialized fare of the Food Network — then in its earliest days - with *Essence of Emeril* and *Emeril Live!*, *Molto Mario*, and *East Meets West with Ming Tsai*. Although we would eventually also become fans of Bobby Flay, his earliest show had a sidekick we just couldn't stand, and so that just wasn't on the viewing schedule. But Mario Batali reigned supreme, for his reverent treatment of Italian food, his jolly and kind personality, and – most importantly – his orange Crocs. It was thanks to those shoes that Papa eventually decided *he* wanted a pair, too, though the ones he purchased were blue, and not official Crocs.

But they were close enough.

We could watch hours upon hours of food television; there were a lot of times when we would see something being made, and decide that it was something easy enough that we could try to do it ourselves. We never actually got as far as putting the recipes into execution, but we did write some of them down. Most of the time, it was because we knew we wouldn't be able to find some of the ingredients around here, others, it was because without the food right in front of us, staring us down, it didn't seem like such a big deal after all. Sometimes it was just more fun to watch the pros at work.

He didn't love watching anyone more than he loved watching Giada DiLaurentiis and Ina Garten. Not only was Giada's focus on Italian cooking – and she was actually Italian! – but she was lovely, and he did, indeed, like pretty people. Ina was calm, soothing, and her cooking bore no hint of the frantic. It was as straightforward and as relaxed as if she wasn't in front of a camera, as if she was just preparing dinner for friends – which she often was - and it seemed like her two favorite things were cheese and chocolate.

Kindred spirits.

***

Food really was an all-around kind of experience for him; he liked making it, he liked eating it, and he liked looking at it. (He even crafted a special fork so that he could maximize the amount of food he could scoop up. With the tines spread out until it looked more like a rake, he was the only person who could actually use that fork. He did it to two of them. I put one in his casket with him.) He liked introducing people to his favorite foods – which is undoubtedly the reason one of my favorite snacks is Locatelli cheese with crackers. In fact, any obnoxiously strong Italian cheese, please hand it over. The more people who will look at me for being crazy for eating it in pieces, the better, and the more delicious I probably think it is. Snacks like that were our after-school tradition, sometimes with pieces of soppressata, sometimes with pieces of prosciutto. Sometimes along with a bowl of soup, or a big plate of salad loaded with vegetables and Ceci beans.

My strangest food habits, and what I think of as being appropriate levels of garlic, and what I like to eat, all of those things come pretty much straight from him. Later, we'll talk a little bit about his love of traveling, which will include a discussion of his love of the Travel Channel. As a result, Andrew Zimmern's *Bizarre Food* will be mentioned. At the end of every episode, the roly-poly host of the Travel Channel show, after eating some exceptionally bizarre food in whatever corner of the world, would give his viewers simple advice:

If it looks good, eat it.

Papa took that advice every day of his life.

chapter seven.
orange is the new navy.

He might have been one of the most capable people in the world when it came to the kitchen, but to be perfectly honest, he wasn't the best at *everything*.

Close.

But not quite.

What wasn't he good at? What was this Superman's Kryptonite? This Achilles' heel? What was the fatal flaw in this hero of epic proportions?

Ask the orange pieces of his wardrobe that started life as some shade of navy-blue. Yes, that's right, the Joker to his Batman was none other than a gallon of bleach.

Either he honestly didn't realize that he had tossed a capful of bleach into a load of laundry that included some colored pieces, or he didn't realize that a piece of colored laundry had snuck its way into an otherwise-white load.

Considering that he was known to just toss dirty clothes into the washer and use it as a hamper of sorts, then put in the detergent and bleach without unloading and sorting sometimes, there's also the possibility that he just didn't care, and was just focusing on getting the clothes washed.

It might have just been that he was so used to needing to bleach something that it had become an automatic reaction. Load of laundry? Capful of bleach.

But why?

Why was he so programmed to automatically toss bleach in?

Papa was a spot-magnet. He could just look at food, and something would get on him. Salad dressing – usually plain canola oil and vinegar – would inevitably splash onto his shirt, doing irreversible damage. Barbecue sauce, spaghetti sauce, pizza sauce, the sauce from his favorite Chinese meals, chocolate ice cream, grape jelly, olive oil from pasta, coffee, tea, pretty much anything you can think of that could get on someone and make a mess? He had done it.

A meal just wasn't complete, and it just didn't feel right, if it didn't involve Papa looking down at his shirt, throwing up his hands, and grumbling "Jeeesus." When Tide-to-Go pens first hit the shelves, we stocked up on them, and started carrying them around with us. Most of the time, we noticed the stains too late for the Tide to do any good – or the new stains had joined old ones that had never quite washed out – so really, while the idea was great in theory, not even portable stain removers were a match for Papa's particular level of spot-attraction.

Considering most of the stains were – of course – on white shirts (it didn't help that most of his shirts were either white, or very light-colored), bleach was an absolute necessity. It might not have been able to completely rid the shirts of their stains, but it could at least fade out the colored stains to a point where they weren't *quite* as noticeable. The idea of having to throw shirts away was awfully disappointing to him – most of the time, because the shirts that got splashed on and spotted were some of his favorites, and he couldn't bear to part with them. (Which explains why some of the shirts in his closet were worn to the point of being nearly transparent, and yet they were still hanging there, complete with little spots on them if you looked hard enough. He was a loyal clothes-owner.)

So, sometimes, bleach was his friend.

But then, it became the Brutus to his Caesar.

***

The first time he pulled a victim of his bleach blunders out of the dryer (because really, who looks at their laundry while it's wet and being transferred at all, let alone pulls the items out for inspection one by one?), he looked quizzically at it. It was one of a pair of dress socks, and he held it out at arm's length, as if it was something that might bite him. "This isn't mine," he said, eyeing the sock. "I don't have orange socks. Is this yours?"

No, it was definitely not mine.

Without much further thought, he set the sock aside and continued unloading the laundry. The other sock – as expected - made its appearance, though this one didn't quite look the same. It was the same pattern, and looked like it was the match to the already-unloaded sock, but the color was off. That one looked almost...paint-splattered. And instead of being completely orange, there were hints of...navy blue?

Uh-oh.

At about the same time I realized what had happened, Papa dropped the sock onto the towel he'd spread across the kitchen table, and glared at the washer, as if the appliance was solely responsible for the transformation of the socks. "God damnit," he grumbled. "Those *are* my socks. They're my *blue* socks."

Well, they used to be.

He grudgingly matched them up, shaking his head all the while. "Damn bleach," he mumbled, going through the rest of his laundry with a critical eye, making sure that no other items of clothing had also fallen prey to the washer's evil plan of laundry domination via the stealth addition of a capful of bleach to the water.

Everything else in the load was fine – clearly, since everything else had been bleachable, considering it was white – and the laundry, including the ruined socks, was carted upstairs and put away. The Case of the Orange Socks had been solved.

But it was just the beginning.

***

Picture this. The setting is the same. The Marocco kitchen, in front of the doors that kept the washer and dryer hidden from sight. Laundry is being pulled from the ancient dryer, ready to be folded. The Case of the Orange Socks appears to have been relegated to the very back corners of our intrepid hero's mind, because there is an ease and a relaxation visible in his actions. As each piece comes out of the dryer, it is met with the usual satisfaction of having a freshly-laundered piece of clothing in one's hands.

Until the shorts.

Papa had a collection of shorts and T-shirts that would have rivaled Imelda Marcos' collection of shoes. When he found something he liked, he bought several, and if they were on sale? So much the better. His favorite shorts were navy blue, and made of sort of the kind of material from which swim trunks are made, though sturdier. They were kind of like a hybrid of swim trunks, warm-up pants, and that fake-denim-y cotton material, if you can imagine that.

And they had just come out of the dryer, no longer navy blue, but a bright, rusty orange, though the stitching was still navy blue. Letting out a howl like a wounded animal, he flung the shorts onto the table, throwing his hands into the air. "I did it again!" he groaned, putting his hands to his head. "My shorts! I *ruined* them! My *favorite shorts!*" He was not to be consoled.

"You can still wear them," I told him, looking at the now-fiercely-orange shorts. "They're not splattery. They're just…orange."

And oh, they were. They were completely, solidly orange.

"I can't wear these!"

"Why?"

"They're *orange!*"

"So are your socks. You can wear them together."

I think, for a second, he seriously considered that. (Since everyone knows only adorable old guys can *really* get away with wearing shorts and high socks. And personally, I'm pretty sure that with my two grandpas, I had the market cornered on adorable old guys. So, I was only half-kidding when I said it.)

With a sigh, he put the shorts on the towel on the table and folded them sadly. "My favorite shorts," he mumbled again, though I noticed that he put them on top of the pile that was destined to go back upstairs and be put back in the dresser.

They might have undergone a bit of an unexpected transformation, and they might not have been the favorite shorts he had come to know and love in the same form, but a little bit of a facelift never hurt anything. It's like when jeans start getting a little bit frayed, and a little bit faded. You don't get rid of them just because they don't look like they did when you bought them. You keep them because they haven't failed you, and it's not like they're riddled with holes that'll make them unpresentable in public.

Orange shorts were a bit unusual, perhaps, but otherwise, they were in perfectly good condition, and he knew that. Whether or not he ever wore them again, they were still his favorite shorts, and they weren't going anywhere anytime soon.

It didn't make him any less grumpy that he'd bleached them, though.

Eventually, the knowledge that his favorite shorts were still upstairs, waiting for him to wear them again despite their new appearance got to him. One day, when I went down to his house, he was sitting on the back porch, newspaper open in front of him, the already-read sections piled on top of the air conditioner, the sections yet to be read in queue, open over the railing, a bottle of his special orange-juice-and-water concoction weighing the already-read sections down against any sudden breeze that might crop up and try to whisk them away.

He was also wearing a very distinctive pair of very orange shorts.

I figured that he was wearing them because he was at home, and he didn't particularly care if any of the neighbors saw the orange shorts. But when we embarked on our adventures for the day – the grocery store, Wal*Mart (also known as one of his favorite places in the world), lunch, our usual routine – he didn't change them.

The number of comments – compliments! – that he received on those shorts that day, and pretty much every subsequent time he wore them, was astounding. It got to the point where he stopped explaining that they really weren't supposed to be that color, that it had all been a terrible mistake, and just started saying "hey, thanks."

He was awfully glad that he'd decided not to throw them away. They were once again cemented as his favorite shorts – especially now that they were different, and there was little to no chance that anyone else would ever have a pair of shorts precisely that color. He wore them so many times that a hole eventually was worn on the outside patch of the back pocket, where he kept his wallet, and there was a little hole on the front bottom hem of the left leg from where it got caught on something, but even then, that wasn't enough to make him stop wearing them.

Sometimes, he even wore them with the orange socks.

It was a fashion statement.

And he was *cool*.

***

There were several other pieces of clothing that would become casualties of the on-going (and losing) war with bleach. One of his many pairs of plaid flannel pajama pants (which were Christmas-gift staples, he loved pajamas) became an odd combination of colors – we're not sure which ones they used to be, because every single color in them warped to something else. They're now a medley of raspberry, orange, and something sort of grey. Countless other pairs of blue socks, and the stitched lettering – but only the lettering – on the sweatshirt we brought him from Little Italy in New York.

You guessed it. The lettering had also once been navy blue.

The funniest thing about the many run-ins with bleach was that he somehow managed rarely to ruin completely any of the pieces of clothing. The occasions when something bore the tell-tale splatters of bleach, a mottled and obvious pattern of the removal of all color, were few and far between. He always managed to bleach things solidly, changing every inch of color there was to be seen, or to bleach only small things, things that wouldn't ever have been noticed if someone hadn't known what color it was supposed to be.

Just as the Joker never *quite* managed to best Batman, even though there were a whole lot of situations when Batman couldn't really say he'd won, bleach never managed to *completely* claim the victory. Papa managed to make the best of his Battle With the Bleach, and he got some really distinctive pieces of clothing out of it, pieces that were one-of-a-kind. Once, we joked with him that he should just throw one of his blazers in the washing machine with some bleach, make himself an orange jacket to go with his shorts and socks.

He lifted his chin imperiously, and looked at us over the rims of his glasses as he shook the newspaper open.

"No. But I would look *great* in an orange jacket," he sniffed.

chapter eight.
big fun with the small screen.

All **of my** strangest habits, all of my favorite things, most of them come directly from Papa. My idea of a perfect snack, my idea of what good music is, my knowledge of how *not* to use bleach, they've all been formed under the influence of that very cool cat. (Or, "handsome devil," as he occasionally liked to point out.)

My taste in television shows, too, comes straight from the Marocco School of Television, and bears the Elmer Stamp of Approval. Of course, *The Price is Right* reigned the eleven o'clock timeslot during the summers, but it wasn't the only thing we made it a point to watch throughout the course of our days together. Some people make sure to watch their "stories" in the afternoon, their schedule crafted around the drama and intrigue of the soap opera set. Ours was scheduled around an eclectic mix of comedies, dramas, talk shows, game shows, and food shows; shows that can't be described as anything but classic, and shows that were new – or at least, currently-running – at the time.

Among other television memories are watching *American Gladiators* at 8:30 in the morning when my mom would drop me off before going to work, then a few years later, coming home from school and watching *Gilligan's Island.* This, of course, is where the comparison to the Skipper and Gilligan began, thanks to my penchant for wearing floppy hats, and his inherent Skipper-ness. We'd watch *Wonder Woman* and *Batman* (the Adam West/Burt

Ward campfest), we'd watch *Rugrats* and *Batman: The Animated Series*. We'd watch *Wishbone*. We'd watch *Everybody Loves Raymond*. We'd watch sports. We'd watch – well, he'd watch – the news. Television was kind of a staple once homework was finished.

***

But the one show that perhaps was "our show" of the lot of them, the one show I have to singlehandedly thank him for introducing me to, is *Night Court*. The zany comedy, which originally aired from 1984-1992, followed the shenanigans of the ragtag crew of legal personnel responsible for dispensing justice in…you guessed it, night court…in New York City. There are some things I can picture and remember as easily as anything, and one of them is being around ten years old, sitting on the end of his old couch, a brown one with a pattern of faded flowers – a couch I once crawled behind like it was a tunnel and sliced my arm open on a nail I couldn't see, which resulted in yet another save-of-the-day from Papa, who fixed me up right away, but with which I had since reconciled for its brutal attack on my four-year-old arm – and settling in for an hour's worth of *Night Court* reruns on A&E at 3:00 in the afternoon.

We laughed at the endearing cluelessness of Bull the bailiff, we'd try to figure out if Judge Harold T. Stone really should have been behind the bench, we'd shake our heads at the antics of ladies' man Assistant District Attorney Dan Fielding, and we'd debate which of the ladies who filled the post of Public Defender over the course of the series was the best addition to the cast. (We decided it was obviously Markie Post's Christine Sullivan.) We would lament the loss of Selma, then the loss of her replacement, Flo, until we finally met Roz, whose take-no-prisoners-but-be-nice-to-Bull attitude was familiar and appreciated, but was still distinctly different than her two predecessors.

My mom couldn't figure out why we bothered, but we didn't care that we were the only ones in the family who would actually watch the show. And then it, like so many shows do, fell victim to the ever-changing schedule of channels, and the re-runs disappeared from the airwaves. (But not before we got to see the series finale, luckily!) I think we may have temporarily replaced it with its replacement, which I think was *L.A. Law*, but that didn't last long. It just wasn't the same.

So when my mom bought me the first season on DVD during my junior year of high school, it was time for a party. Papa and I watched the entire set in the matter of a few days. (The Christmas-themed episode with a young Michael J. Fox has since become necessary viewing every year during the holiday season.) The episodes were as fun as I remembered them being the first time I ever saw them, and of course, it was fun to see ones that I missed during the A&E rerun years. When I found seasons two and three and bought them as a college graduation present for myself, we started watching those too. We only got a few episodes into season two, but what we watched made us laugh. And he stayed awake to watch them, so that adds to the positive memories involving the show.

Most of all, it was fun to just sit with him and laugh mindlessly at admittedly-silly plotlines that were obviously meant to be humorous, and not necessarily reflective of the usually-tense atmosphere of a courtroom. I think that's why we liked it so much; even though we were also avid fans of *Law & Order* and other police-and-courtroom dramas, there was just something refreshing about the shamelessly-silly *Night Court,* and something really lovable about every single one of those characters. They all had their quirks, and all of the actors had their opportunities to showcase their comedic skills. But every once in awhile – like the first-season Christmas episode – there was also a whole lot of heart on display. Hilarious but heartwarming; that was Papa in a nutshell.

***

Bald. Round. A little bit blunt, a little bit offensive in that bluntness. Extremely opinionated, if not entirely informed. Partial to an armchair, not so partial to people telling him what to do. Does that remind you of any particular television character? If you said "Archie Bunker," you'd be right. Another one of the shows to which Papa introduced me was *All in the Family.* And even at a young age, I could sort of see the similarities between Archie Bunker and Papa. Sure, then it was mostly the physical similarities – if Papa's eyes had been blue, and not hazel, and if he hadn't worn glasses, he would have sort of looked like Carroll O'Connor – but as I got older, I realized that there were more than just that they looked alike.

Papa was…blunt. As I described in the preface, "How to Tell a Story," he really didn't care what people thought of the things he said. If he had something to say, he was going to say it. He had opinions, and if other people could go around sharing theirs, there was no reason he shouldn't be allowed to share his, too. He was occasionally so politically incorrect that you couldn't help but laugh – only because you knew that he really wasn't actively trying to be offensive, it just sort of came out that way.

Like when he was talking about baseball. One time, we were sitting at Anna's, and we were discussing some of the new players that had come up to the Pirates. He looked at us from across the table, and shook his head. "Those Dominican Republicans. They could take over the sport." It wasn't meant to be offensive – in fact, we're pretty sure it was a compliment. But it was the use of the phrase "Dominican Republicans" that made us laugh. When we did, he looked at us, his forehead furrowed in confusion. "What?"

"Those what?" my mom asked him.

"Dominican. Republicans," he repeated slowly, as if she just hadn't heard him correctly.

"Dad," she said. "They're not Dominican Republicans, they're just Dominican."

He thought about this for a second, then waved his hand and went back to crumbling saltines into his clam chowder. "Whatever. Dominican Republicans, Dominican, they sure as hell know how to play baseball."

Similarities aside, *All in the Family* was another example of how a show could be responsible for rollicking laughter and also drive home some pretty powerful points. Whether it was using Archie as an illustration of the problems that come from being short-sighted, or bringing to the forefront issues that otherwise might not have been widely talked about at the time, this was a show that could do a lot.

We bought Papa the first two seasons for a "just-because" present several years ago, and as soon as he opened them, he handed me the first season's case. "Put it on!" he crowed, gesturing to the television screen. (He had a very, *very* love-hate relationship with his "TVD" player. Part of it may have come from the fact that where the player was positioned, you had to stand in front of the open cupboard door to get the remote to send the signal, and part of it may have been that he just couldn't be bothered to learn. That was one of the many reasons he had us.) We put the first disc in, and he, my mom, and I watched probably half of it.

The funniest thing was when Papa would shake his head at something Archie said – something that could have just as easily come out of his own mouth – and say "I can't believe he said that." Like Archie, Papa might have been a little bit unaware that sometimes, he shouldn't have said the things he did, but despite those tendencies, he was warm, cuddly, and really very sweet. He definitely loved his family.

***

Kind of like Frank Barone. There wasn't another modern television program that made Papa laugh more than *Everybody Loves Raymond*. He might not have been able to remember what he'd had for lunch the day before, and he might have called us all by the wrong names ("Marmeglynn...raaaaaah!" was not an uncommon outburst.) on occasion, but he could tell you – in picture-perfect detail – what happened in almost any episode. (So what if it was in distinctly-Elmer terms? Amy became "Robert's tall wife" – as if Robert also had a short wife running around somewhere – and the kids were occasionally ignored altogether, but that was fine.)

Despite the fact that he might have been most similar to Frank, Robert was his favorite character. Perhaps it was his perpetual status as runner-up, the occasionally-forgotten child, or any number of the other things that made Robert Barone so very much like a human Eeyore, or maybe it was just that he found Brad Garrett to be a scene-stealer. Whatever the case may have been, he generally remembered episodes according to what happened to Robert, or what Robert did.

Which I'm sure would have pleased Robert – if he weren't just a fictional character – because finally, someone was showing *him* some appreciation.

I don't think there was an episode he didn't see, or that he couldn't identify within a few moments. He could turn any episode on at any point in the action, and settle right in, happy as a lark. He laughed, even when he knew what was coming – perhaps knowing what was coming even made him laugh harder – and listening to him laugh at whatever joke, whatever facial expression, whatever misfortune that had befallen "his boy Robert," was enough to make even the most staunchly-resistant non-comedy-fan laugh right along.

Like *Night Court*, that was probably the most fun thing about watching the show with him. It was the delight that he gained from watching, the fact that it made him laugh – real, belly laughs, not the polite laughter that comes either from knowing you're probably supposed to laugh at that line of dialogue, or from finding something only sort of funny.

Thanks to the reruns on several channels, chances were that he'd be able to find an episode to keep him entertained at any point from six o'clock on, and when the show ended its run a couple of years ago, he depended on those reruns to fulfill his *Everybody Loves Raymond* quota.

Or, as he probably would have preferred, *Everybody Loves Robert*.

***

Papa could identify episodes of *Raymond* within a few minutes. I guess that's where I inherited my ability to do the same with *Law & Order*. One of the few dramas we indulged in, we also tended to use DVD collections to go through the long-running police procedural. (He liked the early seasons, with Chris Noth, and reruns tended to be more from the later years, long after Noth's Logan was exiled to Staten Island for punching a corrupt Congressman and got his own television movie event. So we turned to Seasons 1-5 on DVD, and we didn't even have to deal with commercials.)

Law & Order was one of those shows that while you probably shouldn't say you like it, because of the nature of its content – who likes murder and crime? – we had to say we did. Despite its depiction of the darker side of human nature, the cast was always what set it apart from other police dramas. Led by an undeniable talent like Jerry Orbach for most of its run, with a cast that included the likes of Sam Waterston, Dennis Farina, Steven Hill, Jesse L. Martin, Benjamin Bratt, Jeremy Sisto, Angie Harmon, Jill Hennessy, S. Epatha Merkerson, and Carey Lowell, among many, many others, it was the cast that made you able to say you genuinely liked the show.

Add in that its list of guest stars over its twenty-year run was full of names that were more than notable – Julia Roberts (while not a personal favorite of ours, a notable name indeed), New York mayors Rudy Giuliani and Michael Bloomberg, Tovah Feldshuh, Frances McDormand, Michael Imperioli, and Edie Falco, and you just sort of can't help but acknowledge that the series meant something special to pop culture in general, not just to a duo of fans.

I have a few really good memories that involve *Law & Order*. One is simply the many, many afternoons we spent over Christmas breaks, and the day-long summer marathons watching the DVDs. It was fun to watch him as he became completely engrossed in a case he hadn't seen before, to hear his speculations about who the murderer was and why, his indignant reactions when he didn't think the outcome of the trial was fair, and his appreciation for the dry, witty wisecracks that came out of the mouth of Lennie Briscoe, whom he considered one of his favorite television characters of all time. ("My boy Lennie, always ready with that fast jab!" he'd say with a wit-appreciating grin.)

He also insisted that he'd always seen a connection between Lennie and the equally-sassy medical examiner Elizabeth Rodgers; every time they shared the screen, he'd look at me, serious as could be, and shake his head. "I always thought they would've gotten together," he'd say, pointing at the screen. "They'd have gotten along real well. Third time'd be the charm." (Referring, of course, to Briscoe's two ex-wives, often-mentioned, and much-regretted.) So now, whenever Lennie and Doc Rodgers are on the screen together while I'm watching reruns, if my mom's in the room – which she usually is, we're just a *Law & Order* kind of family – I have to say it. "You know, I always thought they would have gotten together." And we laugh.

One of the others is of when Jerry Orbach died. That night, my dad came home from work, and was sitting at the kitchen table taking off his boots. I was standing at the counter, and he said "So, Jerry Orbach died?"

That was news to me. And of course, I didn't believe him, because usually, any and all *Law & Order*-related news came through me, so if I hadn't heard about it, then it obviously couldn't have been true. I rushed into the living room – not a far rush, really, just a few steps – and my mom had already turned on the news to see if this terrible revelation would be confirmed or denied.

When it was confirmed, there were tears. Lots of them. As ridiculous as it sounds, it was like a member of the family had died. I grabbed the phone, and immediately called Papa.

"Jerry died," I told him. I didn't even have to explain which Jerry I meant, because there was only one Jerry I would be reporting about.

"Aw, man, my boy Lennie. Do you want to come down?" he asked. I said no, and that I'd see him in the morning. The next day, I put on my black *Law & Order* T-shirt, purchased during that summer's trip to New York – a trip during which we saw Lennie Briscoe's trench coat, suit, and tie on a glass-encased mannequin inside the NBC Store at Rockefeller Center – and went down to his house. I was going to the Robinson Mall with Quigley's campus ministry to make Build-a-Bears with the kids from the Women's Shelter, and he was taking me up to the school, where we were all meeting.

When I walked through the door, he was sitting at the kitchen table, coffee in front of him, glasses perched on the end of his nose, toast crumbs on a plate the only remaining evidence of breakfast, newspaper spread out helter-skelter. He was holding the sports section, and the entertainment section was laying in the 'already read' pile. There was a hole at the top of the page, and a neatly-trimmed article sitting alongside it. He had cut out the article about Jerry.

"Our boy. Real, real sad," he said, flipping to the next page of the sports section, and looked at me over the rims of his glasses. "Bring those discs down tomorrow. We'll watch some stuff."

And that was how the annual Jerry Orbach Day of Remembrance came about. For the next six years, every year on December 28th, we would hole up in his living room and watch Jerry's first episode as Lennie, the in-memoriam special features on the Season Three box set, *Beauty and the Beast, Dirty Dancing*, and Jerry's last episode of *Law & Order: Trial By Jury*, which, if you've never seen it, is one of the saddest things in the whole entire world. The episode follows the trial of a man accused of shooting and killing a police officer, and when tensions get too hot, police presence is forbidden from the courtroom. So, as the verdict is being read, Lennie and his fellow officers (though he has, by that point, left the force in order to be a private investigator for the D.A.'s office, a choice necessitated by Orbach's real-life battle with cancer and the need for a lighter workload) are standing outside. Lennie is peering through the crack in the door, and he sees the prosecutors standing up and shaking hands, and he whispers "They got him!" The following conversations are also whispered – because at that point, reports were that Orbach couldn't talk above a raspy whisper, so instead of cutting the lines, the rest of the actors in the scene also decided to whisper.

But we watched everything that marked an important part of his career, and some of our favorite episodes of *Law & Order*. We would also listen to his versions of "Try to Remember," from *The Fantasticks*, "Lullaby of Broadway," from *42nd Street*, "Razzle Dazzle," from *Chicago*, and "I'll Never Fall in Love Again," from *Promises, Promises*. Every year, without fail, that was our December 28th, no question about it.

He even wore his *Law & Order* shirt. And he always knew when it was coming up. "How many years now?" he'd ask, before adding on the correct anniversary number. Even for 2010's anniversary, though by that point, he wasn't in very good shape himself, only a few weeks away from his last hospital stay, he put on that shirt, said it was "six years already, geez," and stayed awake to watch *Dirty Dancing*, and Jerry's last episode of *Trial By Jury*. We cut it short that day, because he was tired, but we got it in.

2011's was pretty bad, because I had two guys to be missing. But in a lot of ways, the reason that the Jerry Orbach Day of Remembrance exists is because Papa suggested it, and while it's obviously not a good memory that now both are gone, it's a good memory that Papa and I shared that tradition of celebrating the life and career of a guy we both admired.

***

Anyone who says that too much television is a bad thing may or may not be right. Too much of anything is a bad thing. But when there are so many shows and television moments that are linked so closely with my memories of Papa, and stories I can tell, I'm going to choose to say that it wasn't about the television, really.

It was about us sharing things we both liked, and spending time together. Whether it was yelling at people for making ridiculous bids on *The Price is Right* ($35,000 for a boat, a car, two trips, and a spa? Really?), cheering on Jack McCoy as he launched a particularly tough line of questions at a witness during *Law & Order*, laughing in disbelief at the latest dopey thing Bull said or did on *Night Court*, shaking our heads at Robert's lack of luck on *Everybody Loves Raymond*, or debating the validity of *Cheers* post-Coach, and post-Diane (we thought Woody was sweet, and while he'd never replace Coach, he was at least entertaining, but Rebecca just wasn't cutting it), we did it together, and we had fun with it.

And I learned about some shows that became my top favorites for forever. Really, he taught me everything I know, even when those things might not be knowledge most people would consider worth having.

Like knowledge of the existence of *Night Court*.

It's necessary.

chapter nine.
how to do a crossword puzzle.

Papa's love-hate relationship with crossword puzzles — any of them, all of them, from the collections of easy ones that can be found in drug stores and newsstands to the *New York Times* — was well-known and the source of a lot of entertainment over the years. When he was finished actually reading the newspaper, he would scour the pages for the puzzle section (that it moved around was yet another source of consternation), until he finally located it. He would carefully cut it out and attach it to his puzzle clipboard, and he would do it every single day. If he didn't finish the puzzle, it would stay on his clipboard, and he would go back to it later in the week.

He swore he never looked at the answer keys that were now in his possession since the next day's puzzle always had the solution for the previous day's puzzle right next to it. He promised he only looked at them when he wanted to check one of his answers.

And his answers were some of the most creative — if hardly correct — in the history of crossword puzzles.

For as long as I can remember, there was a crossword dictionary in the magazine rack in his living room. Even when the magazine rack moved around, you could count on that bright blue dictionary with yellow and white lettering and a crossword grid on the cover being on the bottom level of the rack on the right-hand side. When I was little, I remember asking what kind of book it was, and I had it explained to me that it was to help do puzzles.

At the time, the only puzzles I was aware of were my Barbie "jigsaw" puzzles, and the wooden cut-out sea creatures puzzle I owned. I couldn't figure out why, or how, someone could use a book with lots of words in it to play with one of them. I was then shown, for the first time, a crossword puzzle.

It was *fascinating*. It was also the beginning of what would become a wonderful friendship.

Grandma was always the more avid crossword enthusiast, and the crossword dictionary was hers. (I don't remember Papa ever once picking it up to look for a possible answer. Why should he? He knew everything, and if maybe, by some bizarre stroke of something or other, he *didn't* know, or the word he picked didn't fit, well then…he would *make* it fit.)

My mom inherited the crossword-loving gene, and has always kept a steady supply of Dell crossword books in the house. She, however, is a crossword genius, and only does the hard and expert puzzles. When she had worked her way through them, she took the books down to Papa, and he would happily fill in the easy, and sometimes the medium.

He was one of the smartest guys I knew, so I have no doubt that if he'd wanted to, he could have done the hard ones. His excuse was that there were too many boxes, and the print was too little for him to read when there were that many clues. So in addition to the "hand me down" crossword books, whenever we would find large-print collections of easy crosswords, we would scoop them up and give them to him. (Surprise-presents were even better than "expected" presents.)

His magazine rack was full of crossword puzzle books, in addition to his trusty clipboard full of cut-out-from-the-newspaper puzzles. No matter their origin, they all had one thing in common.

They were filled in with his loopy, distinctive printing, and if they were done in pen, they bore the signs of someone who had changed his mind about a word at least six times, until the letters in the boxes had been written over so many times that not only were they indistinguishable, there was no room left to put any other letters in.

Not to mention, if one studied the boxes hard enough, he or she would see that some of the answers had adopted spellings that satisfied the clue, fit the number of boxes available, *and* somehow fit with one of the other intersecting clues.

Some of them were just absolutely *butchered*.

But he wanted that puzzle to be finished, gosh darn it, and he was going to make that happen any way that he could. (He also employed that approach when it came to Scrabble. If the letters he had on his tile rack made a word that sounded like another word with just a *teensy* bit of a different (read: incorrect) spelling, then he was going to do his darnedest to convince you that it was absolutely acceptable to spell "goofy" as "gufee."

Sometimes, it was literally laugh-out-loud funny what he would come up with.

The best story, though, involves the solving of an actual crossword puzzle. Sometimes, he would leave an unfinished puzzle laying around in the living room. If someone happened to pick it up and help him out? Well, that would be great. Once you were able to decipher which answers were right, and which ones had been morphed and twisted until they looked like they could be right (but weren't!), if you filled in a few boxes for him, he was thrilled.

It was after dinner, and he was in his favorite spot on the couch. My mom was in the armchair, and I was on the other end of the couch. Papa had abandoned the crossword puzzle in favor of reading some of the e-mail jokes my mom routinely printed out for him to read, and he was chuckling to himself every once in awhile.

"Dad?" my mom said, and he looked over.

"What?"

"I don't think this answer is right."

"What answer?" he grumbled. He wasn't wrong.

"This one, right here," she said, unfolding herself from the chair and showing him the newspaper.

He took a second to look at the grid, then at the corresponding clue to the supposedly-incorrect answer. "No, I think it's right," he replied simply, before going back to the jokes.

"I'm pretty sure it's not."

He set the sheaf of e-mails on the arm of the couch, took the newspaper from her, and looked at it more closely. "Five letters. 'Negative response.' 'Noooo.'" His tone was completely serious, cool, and collected. He was dead certain that that was the right answer.

My mom stifled a smile. "You know, I think they're probably thinking it's five different letters. Or at least, not 'noooo.'"

"It doesn't say that. It says five letters. 'Noooo' is five letters."

With that, he picked up the e-mails again, signaling that he was done having that conversation.

I don't remember what the answer actually ended up being. All I know is that it wasn't actually 'noooo,' although his logic made perfect sense. Everyone who's ever heard that story before has gotten a kick out of it, and some of them have even said that now, when they either look at a crossword puzzle, they think of that, or if they hear someone saying 'noooo,' they think of him, too.

Everything I Know

I haven't been able to do a crossword puzzle without laughing since.

***

A love of crossword puzzles is obviously in my blood. When I find myself staring at *The New York Times'* Sunday puzzle, or the daily "Quick Crossword" that's run in the *Pittsburgh Post-Gazette* (which is occasionally harder than the daily *NYT* puzzles, to be perfectly honest), stuck on some answer or another, I try my hardest to actually figure it out, whether I have to ask my mom, turn to the Internet, or some other source of information.

But every once in awhile, when there's that one, pesky square that's preventing me from completing the puzzle because I have no idea what either of the clues involving it are, I'm awfully, awfully tempted to just fill in a letter that makes both parts of the grid into words.

It's probably what he would have done. [2]

---

[2] As a result of my inability to write a book in order, I skipped around, writing chapters as I felt inclined to write them, depending on the story I wanted to tell on any given day. Chapter Nine was the last to be written, and so this was the last page that needed to be completed. Please note the page number. It's one of his favorite numbers.

chapter ten.
have remote, will travel

When I was little, Papa and Grandma, and their best friends Frank and Jo Costentine, would take a trip to Las Vegas. It was one of Papa's favorite places, although his number-one destination was San Francisco – "the most beautiful city in the world," while also being "the land of fruits and nuts." (Offense isn't, and really wasn't, meant. He was just...colorful.) I can vaguely remember going to pick them up from the airport once, and then I definitely remember going to pick him up after the few trips he made by himself.

Even after Grandma died in 1995, he still hightailed it out to Sin City every year for a couple of years, usually with his friends from Our Lady of Fatima, who arranged an excursion. His last trip was in the early 2000s, and it was on that trip that he came home with tales of having met George Foreman in the hotel elevator. ("He was *big*!" was his surprised comment. How this was a surprise was anyone's guess, but he was excited to share it.)

He always came home with great stories.

His favorite one, however, one that he told over and over, was also from that same last trip. His traveling companion, his best (adult male) friend Frank (with whom he shared the mutual nickname "Hop") ended up not making the trip, after getting sick on the way to the airport, and so Papa found himself in the airport by himself, without a specific traveling buddy. As he walked up to the check-in counter, the agent on the other side looked at him and said "You know, you remind me of this man I know, from Aliquippa, a Mr. Marocco…"

At that point, she glanced down at his information, looked back up at him, and shouted "You *are* Mr. Marocco!" She scrambled out from behind the counter to give him a hug.

(He loved hugs, and he gave the best ones in the whole world.)

After the hug, the agent – who shall remain nameless, but knows who she is, and how much he loved her! – went back to her post on the other side of the counter, and looked down at his information again.

And she upgraded him to first class.

After thanking her profusely – with a few more hugs - , he made his way to the gate, where he sat with the rest of the group and their fellow Vegas-bound fliers. He didn't tell anyone about his good fortune; instead, he sat there with his newspaper as if there was nothing different about his flying plans at all. As the gate attendants began making boarding announcements, and called for first-class passengers to begin boarding, he stood, stretched, casually looked at his church-friends, and said "Oh, that's me."

And he boarded the plane with a grin. When he got home a few days later, he was full of hilarious stories about the reactions the others had had when they reconvened after the plane landed at McCarran. "How did you manage that one?" was the most-asked question, and his response – according to him in the retelling, which may or may not have been the real answer; we've established that he was a Grade-A storyteller, and sometimes, he liked to embellish to make things more exciting – was "I happen to be famous."

Actually, it's entirely possible that that really was, actually, his reply.

He told that story so many times over the next few years, and thanked the agent profusely every single time he saw her after that. "You know, I flew first class to Las Vegas," he'd say, and we'd listen as he launched into the tale yet again. It was one of those stories that, just as it never really got old for him to tell it, it never got old to listen to, either. For that to have happened on that particular trip, one that started out in a less-than-pleasant way with Big Frank getting sick, and leaving Papa without his buddy, was the best way to make it better. For that to have been his last memory of going to Vegas? Even better.

I think that would be considered a jackpot.

***

Right after my graduation from high school in 2006, we – my mom, my aunt and uncle, my great-aunt, Papa, and I – took a trip to Florida to celebrate my graduation, the graduation of my cousin in Florida, Father's Day (which fell on the Sunday we would be leaving Florida), and just to sneak in an unofficial sort of reunion with the Florida contingent of the family.

We also took the opportunity to visit Deland, Florida, where Papa was stationed for a time during his stint in the Navy. After having lunch in a little Italian restaurant in the quaint and picturesque small town – where he charmed the proprietress -, we wandered around for a little bit, checking out the shops that lined the street, pausing every once in awhile for a photo opportunity. When we finally tired of the shopping-tourist routine, we moved on to the real point of making our way to the former base town.

Papa wanted to show us the base itself.

Armed with a map, we drove to where the base had been. What we found was something that looked vaguely like it *could* have been a Navy base at one time, but was definitely not active anymore. After asking around, we found out that the base had been decommissioned not long after he left, but that the building that used to be the quartermaster's house had been turned into a small museum that was open to visitors. So we drove up to the little building, and walked in.

The man on duty was named Charlie, and he was an Army veteran. The museum was mostly run by volunteers, and that day happened to be his. Papa explained that he had been stationed at Deland, gave him the timeframe of his assignment, and Charlie looked through the records. He managed to locate one of the other men who had been stationed there at the same time as Papa was, and he called him up on the telephone right there in the middle of the museum. Papa talked to the man for about half an hour, and when he hung up, he had the biggest smile in the world on his face.

We spent a good part of that day just meandering around the museum; despite its size, it was packed full of memorabilia, from photographs and correspondence of and between the men who had been stationed there (and we're pretty sure we spotted a young Papa in one of the group shots, though it was a little bit blurry and affected by age), to general-World War II-era stuff and actual uniforms that had been donated. Papa was in his element, reminiscing about the time he spent there, and trading stories with Charlie about what it had been like to be in the service then.

By the time we left, he had put his name on a mailing list for a newsletter that would allow him to keep up with the news about his fellow sailors, he'd had an hour and a half or so of conversation with Charlie – we had been the only ones in the museum – and he'd gotten to relive the years he spent there. We'd gotten to see some incredible memorabilia, and watch his face while he took everything in.

He'd also gotten a T-shirt, a hat, and I'm pretty sure he got a free window cling. And, as we all now know, there wasn't much that he liked more than getting free things.

He wore the T-shirt so many times over the next few years that it ended up getting a tiny hole near the collar, and of course, had been liberally dotted with various stains, but he couldn't have been prouder to wear it, and to have people ask questions about its origin when he did.

He might never have served overseas, but he sure was proud to have been in the Navy, and to have served where he did. We have lots of pictures of him in uniform: some of them are of him clowning around with his friends, looking like a behind-the-scenes shot of a production of Rodgers & Hammerstein's *South Pacific,* and then we have some of him posing, the quintessential portrait of the serious sailor. It was never a case of us not knowing he served, but to have been on base – decommissioned though it may have been – was a really wonderful experience.

And they had a fighter jet right outside.

That was pretty cool.

The rest of that trip was nice, too, because he got to spend time with nieces that he didn't always get to see. To have the Fusco girls (the daughters of my grandmother's brother) all gathered in one place with their families, and to be able to celebrate a whole bunch of things at one time – Kalie's graduation, my graduation, and Papa's eightieth birthday, among other things – was the basis for a really wonderful couple of days. That was the last plane trip he took, and on our way down?

My aunt paid to upgrade his ticket to first class.

He'd done it again.

***

When my mother, aunt, uncle, great-aunt and I went to New York City the summer before I turned sixteen, Papa didn't come with us – "What the hell do I want to go to New York for?" was his response – but we called him every night to update him on our adventures, and just to check in. One night, as we were making our way back to the hotel after seeing *42nd Street* with Patrick Cassidy, my mom looked up at the *Good Morning, America* marquee flashing over Times Square. She got a big smile on her face, and looked at me. "Let's call Papa and tell him we just saw Connie Chung."

Okay, before I go any further, maybe I should explain. Papa thought women of Asian descent were the most beautiful women in the world. That might be part of the reason he was so fond of Ana, and it's definitely the reason he had a little bit of a thing for Yoko Ono. (It definitely wasn't because he was a fan of the Beatles, save for "Let it Be," and "Imagine," though the latter was, of course, not the Beatles, but John Lennon.) And Connie Chung, as far as he was concerned, was the most beautiful of all.

Now that you have the backstory – even though I can't explain it any further than that – we can continue.

"Let's call Papa and tell him we just saw Connie Chung."

So we dialed his number, even though it was closing in on eleven o'clock at night. We knew he'd be up, probably watching *SportsCenter*. When he picked up, we greeted him with "Guess what!"

"What?"

"We just saw Connie Chung!"

We had to stifle snickers. Luckily, there were still so many people on the street that it wouldn't have been hard to cover them up, even if the phone was right next to our heads.

There was a pause, one we expected to have been borne of absolute excitement. Instead, we got a flat, but very definite, response of "…no you didn't."

"We did!" we tried again, but once again, what we thought had been a brilliant ruse failed.

"No, you didn't."

"How do you know that?"

"Because it's her birthday. She's in California with that pig," he replied with nothing short of total certainty. His matter-of-fact reply brought about another round of laughter, and he chuckled, too.

We're still not sure why, or how, he knew that it was Connie Chung's birthday, and even though that knowledge meant that we weren't able to convince him we'd seen her, it supplied us with one of our best "Elmer Stories."

After catching him up on what we'd done that day, and giving him a review of the show (during which he may or may not have given a little warble of "Lullaby of Broadway"), we told him we'd see him the next day at some point, and we hung up.

We relayed the conversation to my aunts and uncle, and my mom shook her head again. "I can't believe he knows it's her birthday, and where she is, on top of that."

We probably shouldn't have been surprised.

He knew everything.

***

It wasn't only far distances that he traveled, or that we had to travel and report back to him, to get good stories. For a couple of years, every Friday night, he would get together with a group of other old guys and play poker. They didn't play very far from our house at all, but it was his weekly outing, and he looked forward to it – even though he complained about losing money to "those old grumps" more often than he boasted about winning.

But you can bet that when he won, we did hear about it.

In addition to those Friday night poker games, there were a few smaller jaunts that he took that were noteworthy. When Barbra Streisand – his goddess – came to Columbus, Ohio for a concert, my aunt and uncle bought him a ticket, and they took him, and they made a weekend out of it.

When he came home, he was floating on air.

"We were waiting, and waiting, and then the lights went out, and then," he paused, and sighed deeply, as if he was witnessing a miracle of God, "*there she was*. She just…there she was. And I was *right there*. Barbra. I cried." We had no doubt that that was true; he owned almost every album she'd ever cut, and for him to have seen her, live in person, was a dream come true for him. He kept the program and his ticket tucked away, in near-perfect condition. He talked about that concert for days, possibly weeks.

We're so happy that he got to see her.

The last noteworthy excursion was the year his Christmas present was for a weekend at Nemacolin Woodlands. He had been saying that he wanted to go, wanted to see it, wanted to know what the big deal was. So my aunt and uncle, again, made reservations, and whisked him away for a weekend. When he came home, he was loaded down with tales of the luxury in the rooms, the sheer amount of things there were to do, and sweatshirts for me and my mom.

The gifts he was most excited about?

The tiny bottles of lotion and shampoo that he'd stashed in his suitcase. These, he presented to us with all the fanfare that might have been accorded the crown jewels. Those little bottles are still in our medicine cabinet, and whenever we see travel-size things like that in bathrooms in hotels, we laugh.

It was always the little things he liked best.

***

And when traveling just wasn't an option anymore, for various reasons, he turned to the television to take him places he'd never been, or to revisit places that had made their marks on his life. It was the summer of 2010 when the Travel Channel really became a staple of the daytime television schedule in Casa Marocco, and so, it was the summer of 2010 when I was introduced to the likes of Anthony Bourdain – "it's time for my boy Tony!" Papa would exclaim in delight – and Andrew Zimmern, who would eat things not even a courageous eater like Papa would have touched. With those two, and with the other series and specials that the Travel Channel had to offer (like the ones where they would count down the top ten most incredible houseboats or something), we traveled all around the world, experiencing cultures and foods and ideas that we otherwise probably never would have seen or heard of.

So maybe we only did it from the couch in his living room, but it was fun, and it was extremely educational – who knew there were that many places in the United States that were solely famous for hot dogs or hamburgers? – but most of all, it was something that we did together. And now, whenever I watch *No Reservations* or *Bizarre Foods*, I think about how excited Papa would be whenever either of them came on. With *Bizarre Foods*, he would theorize about what Andrew would eat that day, and where he would be. With *No Reservations*, he would happily mimic the introduction, make an inevitable comment about the volume of Tony's alcohol consumption throughout the course of the episode, and laugh at his snide, snarky, witty, and dry narration.

But he would also give an impressed nod when the tough-as-nails former chef showed a softer side, one that wasn't so rebel-without-a-cause. The Lebanon episode will forever be one that sticks with me, not only for Tony we saw in the episode itself, and the absolutely terrifying situations that played out on the screen, but for Papa's reaction to it. He was completely silent throughout the entire thing, and when it was over, he quietly changed the channel.

He might not always have been the most tactful person in the world, and he definitely had his Archie Bunker moments where what he said really wasn't very politically correct. But the way he reacted to the Lebanon episode of *No Reservations*, and the fact that it was, essentially, a wholly unscripted episode that dealt frankly with a very real, very sensitive subject, was just one of the many moments you realized that he really did have the biggest heart in the world, and seeing something like that played out on-screen made him really, really sad.

So when the next episode we saw was Tony, back to normal, as he trotted around the globe and gave viewers an inside look of cultures while brandishing his usual sword of sarcasm, Papa was happy again. And when the Travel Channel wasn't one of the stations available on the television in the hospital?

He had no reservations about telling the nurses just what he thought about *that*.

chapter eleven.
golf isn't so bad.

As a little girl at five years old, there was nothing more boring than than the idea of a bunch of old guys using funny-looking metal sticks to hit a very, very tiny little white ball into a very, very tiny hole.

Real golf was nothing like putt-putt, which was obviously *way* cooler. *Those* golf balls were fun colors like blue and red and purple, and some even had stripes, and there were fun things like windmills and loop-the-loops to hit the ball through, and this was just…

…Dull.

I think I also disliked the notion of golf because I knew that it was the reason that, on Tuesdays during the spring, summer, and early fall months, I didn't get to hang out with Papa. He belonged to two different golf leagues – both with all his cool old-guy friends, all of whom I liked quite a bit – and they went every Tuesday, without fail, to Beaver Creek Meadows in Calcutta, Ohio.

That was *so far away.*

That was practically Calcutta, *India.*

So, I had a problem with golf that had nothing to do with what five-year-old me perceived as an utter lack of action. My biggest problem with golf was that it cut into my Papa-time, and that just wasn't okay.

76

Not to mention, I just couldn't understand what was so fun about walking around a very boring-looking golf course, carrying a very heavy bag, and having to hit a ball very far.

And for all of my confusion about why he wanted to go and do all of those super-boring things every single Tuesday when the weather was nice and he could, instead, be playing with me on the back porch, listening to music, coloring, feeding the squirrels, doing jigsaw puzzles, eating cheese and crackers, or sitting in the yard on the old paint-splattered sheet we used as a "picnic blanket," the biggest, most confounding thing of all was how *watching* it on television could possibly be more fun than watching cartoons.

Maybe I could have seen that playing it might be a little better, because at least then you were actually participating. (And once, Papa gave me an old golf club to play with in the back yard. When I joyfully hit a ball, and it bounced off the tree and came ricocheting back at me? That was my last foray into the world of golf that wasn't contained in the relative safety of a miniature golf course.) But to watch it on television, with no actual involvement, and the whispering broadcasters, and the quiet, and the funny clothes…that was *torture*.

But he liked it, and with all the time we spent watching things I liked, he had to have some time to watch the things he liked, too. Plus, if golf was on, that meant that I could take a nap without worrying about missing anything really, really important.

There were a few things I guess that I *did* like about golf, though. One was the clothes. Those funny pants, and the hats that looked like the ones Papa always wore — and that will never not be inextricably associated with him in my mind — and the sweaters and the shoes and the high socks? They were the greatest.

I also liked some of the players. Obviously, Arnold Palmer was a name I knew. I also recognized names like Fuzzy Zoeller (his name was *Fuzzy*. It sounded like a Muppet!), and Payne Stewart (because of the fact that he wore the cool clothes, and because I remember Papa being so upset when Stewart died), and I recognized hats like Greg Norman's. For several holidays in a row (including birthdays), we bought him Don Wade's series of books, the first of which was *And Then Jack Said to Arnie…*, followed by *And Then Arnie Told Chi-Chi…, And Then Chi-Chi Told Fuzzy…, And Then Fuzzy Told Seve…, And Then Seve Told Freddie…*, and the last one we bought him was *And Then Freddie Told Tiger*, though the series continued for a few books after that. They were collections of anecdotes, told by golfers (and not just the titular ones, all kinds of golfers), light-hearted reads featuring his favorite players.

It all started because the first two involved Arnold Palmer's name. And then he liked them, so it snowballed. I wish I knew what happened to that collection, because most of them are out of print, but it was just another example of how much he liked golf. Not only could he watch it on TV, he could *read* about it.

I think that's where I get my tendency to defend fiercely the value of baseball, whether it's live, on television, in a documentary, or in a book. People think baseball's boring? I don't think they've ever really watched a game. That was how Papa felt about golf. One day, when I was sitting on the couch with him, I didn't have anything else to read while he was watching a golf match, so I picked up *And Then Jack Said to Arnie...* and flipped it open.

The stories were *great*. These guys – guys who looked so serious as they traipsed around the links, doing their painstakingly precise thing – were *hilarious*. I read a little of that book every afternoon after that, and started paying attention to the players more as matches were broadcast on television. Now that I knew a little bit more about them as people, and the kinds of personalities they had, it was a little more interesting.

I still couldn't figure out what most of the purpose of the sport was, other than to prove that you could tap a golf ball in with as much care as you could hit it really, really hard, and really, really far, but it was a little more interesting once the players became a little bit more than just faces with names. (And cool clothes.)

Years trickled by, and I eventually found myself actually paying attention to golf when it was on television instead of finding something else to do. I recognized players readily, could tell you a little bit about how they were playing in any given match, and some of them, I even actively cheered for. One of them, of course, was Arnie. The other was Phil Mickelson, who, for whatever reason, had endeared himself to me. I was slowly learning about the sport: what the scores actually meant, that it wasn't a good thing when someone ended up in the sand, and, most importantly, that sometimes, alligators really do hang out on golf courses. In addition, I had come to realize that the courses I'd once thought were so terribly boring-looking were actually outstandingly beautiful, and that there's not much that's more breathtaking than Augusta National in the springtime.

When he stopped golfing with the guys from church – for various reasons, the group had dwindled to a number that made it a little bit pointless (pointless isn't the right word, though) to try to assemble and go – he gave his golf clubs away, and then, he seemed to place even more importance on being able to watch the tournaments on television.

The year Arnie hit his last shot at Augusta during the Masters before his retirement, Papa got super-emotional at the dinner table on Easter Sunday, which usually seems to coincide with the Sunday of the Masters. Forget family conversation at the table after dinner. He would be right back in front of the television, bellowing at bad shots, cheering when the player he'd touted as the sure-fire winner took one more step to proving him right, and pointedly ignoring anyone who tried to interrupt his golf-viewing.

It was serious business, okay?

Once I had become a convert to the world of a golf fan, and the more I learned about the players as players, and the way they played the game, Papa and I would debate. They weren't super-golf-knowledge debates by any means. I didn't know how to spot a flaw in a swing – and I still don't, unless it's glaringly obvious – and I couldn't judge how much backspin would sink a putt from nine feet out when the hole was in the southwest corner of the green, or anything like that, so I just sort of threw out opinions on whether or not I liked someone, explained why, and he would either agree or refute.

Most of the time, we just lamented over what seemed to be Phil Mickelson's tendency to collapse on Saturdays despite thrilling, spectacular play on Thursdays and Fridays, complained that we were tired of seeing the same player win *everything* (and when that particular player hit rock-bottom as some bad behavior was made public, there may have been a certain amount of glee that finally, there might just be a chance for some fresh blood to start making names for themselves), and commented on the questionable wardrobe choices of some of the players.

Ian Poulter's pink pants (which prompted us to rename him Ian Pinkpants, creatively enough), and John Daly's outrageously-patterned and ridiculously-loud pants in various and sundry patterns and colors were very often topics of discussion. Most of the conversations involving Daly's distinctive style invariably circled back to observations about the golfer's fluctuating weight. When he was on the slimmer side, Papa would nod approvingly – not unlike his response to Drew Carey's shrinking waistline – and say "My boy John's looking good." When he was on the upswing, he'd shake his head. "Shouldn't be wearing pants with that much on them," he'd note.

We could have hosted *What Not to Wear: The PGA Edition.*

***

It's thanks to Papa, and hours upon hours of sneaky conditioning to like golf, that I'll happily sit in front of the television and watch golf matches. I love the Masters – a lot of that has to do with the course itself, because again, I don't think there's much that's prettier than Augusta, especially on a beautiful, sunny day when everything's in full bloom – and I love watching the U.S. Open.

The Open (the British one!), not so much. It's usually raining. And watching those poor guys trudging around a muddy golf course in rainy old Europe – no matter how historic the golf course is – while battling wind, rain, and a whole lot of rain gear is depressing. (I'm also not a fan of the Ryder Cup, because I inevitably end up having to cheer against someone I like, and that's too much work.)

Golfers should look jaunty, gentlemanly, like they should be saying "jolly good day today, isn't it?"

Not like walking garbage bags who would rather be anywhere but where they are. And no matter how bad I feel for them for having to walk around in that weather (I don't care if they're getting paid to do it, that's *gross*), it pales in comparison to how bad I feel for the caddies. So, if it's raining and play's continuing? I'd rather not watch. Call me back when the sun is shining, and the players are happily interacting with the fans as they wind their way through the course on their way to the eighteenth hole.

Speaking of interaction with the fans, that was something Papa always said fascinated him. He always said that he'd never really seen players be so approachable as they've become in recent years, and that it was something he was really glad had changed. Sure, there had always been a few exceptions to the rule, but even the exceptions were mostly stoic and serious when they were in the middle of a match. In addition, he'd never seen fans react to players the way they do now; instead of the polite, almost-aristocratic air of galleries past, there is loud cheering, elated cries of the names of favorite players, sometimes-unbridled joy rolling in waves from the throngs of people flanking the course.

Forget being silent observers; it's a sport. The people are there to see the players they love playing the game they love, and they're going to make sure that the players are aware of their appreciation.

And sometimes, their complete and utter disdain, which occasionally made Papa laugh more than it should have. He liked to watch the way the players being heckled would respond to their critics, as long as they tried to ignore them and pretend like they weren't there. If they reacted negatively, whether by getting caught saying something by an observant camera, or by shooting dirty looks at the gallery, or by making wounded and aggressive comments in post-match press conferences, he would get so upset. There wasn't much that he disliked more than seeing that sort of behavior; he believed that, as professional athletes, they needed to be able to shake off the fact that sometimes, people weren't pleased with their play, to ignore it, smile, and move on.

He also knew that sometimes, it was just the golfer's frustration with himself coming out in a misdirected way. But honestly, I think he had a sixth sense when it came to knowing which players were genuinely kind, likable guys, and which ones had attitude problems. And if one of his guys disappointed him by behaving badly? He would look like one of his family members had just been sentenced to life in prison. Consistent whiners weren't on his list of people to watch, and while he was generally happy with the "new" PGA, with all of the fresh new faces, there was never going to be anyone who would compare with the men who really helped to bring the sport to a level of prestige here in the States. (According to his opinion, of course.)

Arnold Palmer and Jack Nicklaus wouldn't ever be topped. Not by upstarts, not by genuinely good players who were following in their footsteps, and not by flashes in the pan. His loyalty would always be to those guys, though he was also partial to Fred Couples ("my boy Freddie!") and Jim Furyk (simply because he's a Pittsburgh boy, and is known to wear black and gold.) When my mom and I went to the Pirates game that celebrated Arnie's 80th birthday, I recorded the video messages that played on the Jumbotron during inning breaks, and the pre-game festivities so that he could watch them.

(After he got his bobblehead, of course.)

Arnie was still the king.

I couldn't disagree.

***

Golf may not be my number one sport, and I may not know how to play. (I also don't really have any desire to learn how to play, because let's face it, I would need golf clubs crafted for a five-year old.) But I like it a whole lot better now than I did when I was little, and whenever I sit in front of the television to settle in to watch a match, I'm grateful that the lesson finally sank in.

Golf really isn't so bad.

chapter twelve.
and so i reach my final curtain.

It was December of 2010. After a year's worth of trips in and out of the hospital, first for pneumonia (and a piece of cauliflower that had somehow ended up in his lung, long story), then for a resurgence of the Congestive Heart Failure that had plagued him for years, and a short stint in a rehab facility so that he could regain the strength lost from extended stays in the hospital (and shoddy care from said hospital, whose staff was content to let a pneumonia patient stay in bed instead of getting him up and moving around), he had come home, and had been there for about a month.

But everything was different.

Instead of the bold, sassy, and energetic Papa I knew, the Papa who was responsible for the best memories of my life, there was a tired, tiny man who could no longer drive – something which had always given him a lot of pleasure – or even really move around without at least some help.

There was a man who just looked like he was ready to say goodbye, but didn't want to admit it.

And I watched it happen. I watched for two months as his resistance crumbled, as he came to terms – before the rest of us were even ready to acknowledge it – with the fact that time was almost up. I sat with him every day, and I watched television with him, and I had breakfast, lunch, and dinner with him, and I helped him with the exercises his various therapists had taught him.

When he wanted to do them, which wasn't often. He just preferred to sleep.

And that was the hardest thing in the world.

Christmas Eve 2010 was the first one that the whole family didn't spend together; Papa just wasn't up to going out to my uncle's house. So my mom and I stayed with him and the three of us had dinner at his kitchen table – the place where the first Christmas Eve I can remember happened. We had dinner after he instructed me how to prepare the baccala that we were sending with my other uncle; he sat at the table while I cut the fish into pieces, and...

Well, I can't really tell you what I did, because I already told you, I can't tell you the recipe.

It's still a secret.

But I listened as he told me what to do, a master passing along the torch. Once my aunt, uncle, and cousin came by to pick up the baccala and drop off a tray of cookies, my mom and Papa and I sat down to a dinner of spaghetti with sauce homemade by my aunt, and it was the first of the last two dinners that he really seemed to enjoy. The second came on Christmas Day, when I made him homemade baked macaroni and cheese. I had told him that his Christmas present was going to be a meal of whatever he wanted; he just needed to say the words, and I'd make it all. And what he wanted was macaroni and cheese.

So he got macaroni and cheese, plus grilled chicken, and baked pears for dessert.

That he ate two plates worth, and told me how much he enjoyed it, was the best Christmas present I ever could have asked for. I'm so glad, and so grateful, that I was there with him for his last Christmas, and that, for just two days, he was all there, and was mostly the "real" Papa.

New Year's Eve was the last night that I think I can really say that happened. He sat up with us and played Pinochle with my mom and my aunt – and remembered the rules better than they did, and beat them both soundly in almost every hand – and laughed and snacked, and then watched the Friday-night rerun of a noteworthy Pirates game from the 2010 season.

Just a few days later, my mom and my uncle came home from a doctor's appointment with him, and my mom told me that the doctor thought we were coming to the end. And then, about a week later, maybe two, Papa woke up from a nap on his couch, sat up faster, and with less help than he'd needed in awhile, and said that he was having trouble breathing. After a few minutes of sitting up – and a vehement denial that he needed the ambulance to come – he said that he felt better, and he laid back down.

He sat up again a few minutes later, and this time, the ambulance-denial wasn't as sure.

The paramedics came, and they made the decision that, whether or not he wanted to – he hated that hospital, he hated it with a passion – they were going to take him to the emergency room.

That was the last time he would be in his house.

The very next day, when we went to visit him at the hospital, it was obvious that something was different. He had very little idea of where he was, and coherency fluttered in and out. According to the nurse, that sometimes happened with dementia patients; as long as they were in a familiar environment, they were mostly okay. But when that familiarity was taken away, so were the last vestiges of coherency.

We had suspected for awhile that he was in the beginning stages of the disease, but to see its effects without the buffer of his home and things he knew and loved was…hard. When he looked at me like a stranger that night as I stood at the foot of his bed, I thought my heart was breaking.

How could he not have known who I was? I was his sidekick for twenty-two years, his partner in crime for shopping, mischief, music, and television-watching. I was the Gilligan to his Skipper. I was the Batgirl to his Batman.

I was his girl.

But at the same time, it almost made it easier, in a horrible, horrible way.

It wasn't unusual to watch him suddenly start staring off into the distance, to pick a spot on the wall and focus on it as if he was seeing something really, really wonderful and fascinating. A couple of times, he talked as though he was reliving some other part of his life, mentioning things that made no sense to us, but that you just knew made absolute sense to him. And then there were the moments when he was completely lucid, but dreamy.

One of those moments was the moment we knew, for certain, that it was almost time to say goodbye. He was laying in the hospital bed, staring at the wall, transfixed. "Wow," he whispered, smiling, "they did a really nice job on that bar."

"What bar?" my mom asked him.

"That bar back there. Cherry. Then over there, there's a patio, and over there, there's a dance floor. Wow, those boys did really nice work."

"Who are you dancing with?" was my aunt's question, and a thoughtful expression played across his face.

"I'm not sure, but the last time I saw her, she was crippled."

Before my grandmother died, she was wearing a back brace, and was pretty much confined to a wheelchair.

After about two weeks in the hospital – two weeks during which we couldn't be sure if he would even know who we were – he was able to get a bed in the Villa St. Joseph, a care facility run by the Sisters of St. Joseph in

Baden, Pennsylvania. He moved in on February 8th, the day after the Steelers lost to the Green Bay Packers in Super Bowl XLV. On February 12th, my mother called me from the Villa and told me that her friend was on her way to pick me up.

When we got to the Villa and into his room, everyone was standing around; he had stopped talking, and we could literally hear the fluid as it built up inside him. But he was smiling, and he was waving, and he was giving kisses and hugs from his bed like there was no tomorrow.

We weren't sure there was.

But I walked in, and my mom said "Look who's here!" and he lit up.

And a heart that was broken, and continuously-breaking, got a little bit of a Band-Aid.

We all sat there for awhile, debating if we wanted to go home or not, if going home would just mean getting a call once we were there and having to double back. That night ended up not being the last one, but we all went home knowing that there weren't many left.

The next day, February 13th, we were all in his room: his sons and their wives, his daughter, his sisters-in-law, his brother, his grandchildren, and even his cleaning lady, who had brought him a Valentine of Reese's peanut-butter hearts that she had promised him when she'd cleaned his house the month before. The staff at the Villa couldn't have been more wonderful as we all piled in, and supplied us with a cart stocked with drinks and snacks so that we didn't have to leave to get them.

We sat there all day, and over the course of those few hours, it became obvious; he wasn't going to be getting better. His oxygen level was steadily decreasing, and we could hear the fluid level increasing. Around 10:30 that night, my aunts left after some discussion with the nursing staff, and the rest of the family. The nurse in charge told us that sometimes, patients will hang on because they know the family's around, that sometimes, it's easier for them to let go when there aren't a whole lot of people around. So my mom, her brothers, and my great-aunt and I stayed, even after my aunts and cousins went home.

At a little past eleven-thirty that night, Papa's eyes opened for the first time all day, and he stared, smiling, at the top corner of the room. After a few minutes, the room became quiet; the gurgling, the labored attempts to breathe, had stopped.

He was gone.

But he was smiling.

And I have no doubt that where he was now, he was dancing again, sweeping onto the floor to take his Valentine for a long-awaited spin.

When we got home that night, I finished work on the obituary that I had been writing, and the next day, I sent it to the funeral home. That Tuesday, the 15th, it appeared in the newspaper, to let people know the arrangements for the visitation and the funeral. Those details were added after it left my possession, so this isn't the "official" copy; this is what it looked like when it left me.

"On February 13, 2011, Elmer David Marocco, beloved father, wonderful grandfather, protective brother, loving uncle, devoted cousin, and loyal friend, entered into Eternal Life. A proud Navy Veteran and 'railroad man,' Elmer was a member of St. Titus Roman Catholic Parish in Aliquippa, where he was also a member of the Holy Name Society and a "retired" member of the "Titan Hall Crew," having served as maitre'd for many years. In addition to his role in the parish, he was a past president of the A&S Railroad Federal Credit Union in Hopewell Township, a 4th Degree Knight of Columbus, and a past president of the Board of Directors for Linmar Homes, where he lived for fifty years. His proudest accomplishment, however, was his family. A genuinely kind and humble man, he influenced the lives of everyone he met for the better, and regaled them all with wonderful stories every step of the way.

Preceded in death by his parents Eleuterio, Theresa, and Maria, brothers Dominic, Bobby, Danny, and James, sisters Margaret, Gloria, Maria, and Eleanor, brothers-in-law Ed Opsatnik, Bob Borsani, Charles Cater, Skip Dzvonar, Jack Sheldon, and Anthony Fusco, sisters-in-law Betty Iacobucci and Betty Fusco, cherished friends Frank and Josephine Costentine, and the love of his life, wife Connie, he is survived by his children Christine Taylor, David and Michael Marocco, and Marianne O'Neill, sons- and daughters-in-law Arthur Taylor, Diana and Michele Marocco, and Andrew O'Neill, brother Frank Marocco, sisters Dora Dzvonar, Tina Sheldon, Eleanor Cater, and Mamie Bertram, sisters-in-law Nancy Marocco and Lynn Fusco, grandchildren Megan O'Neill, Natalie, Nico, and Isabella Marocco, many well-loved nieces and nephews, and long-time physician and friend Dr. Amar J. Singh.

In lieu of flowers, the family requests donations to the Sisters of St. Joseph/the Villa St. Joseph."

When the day of the funeral visitation finally rolled around — we had chosen to do one day, a four-hour time slot, instead of two days at two hours each — we got to the funeral home at about quarter to four.

There were already people there.

By the time the clock ticked around to 4:05, the line of visitors was out the door, and that flow never slowed down. People willingly stood in a two-hour line. Despite the fact that we asked people not to send flowers, the viewing room was full of beautiful arrangements, and that night, eight hundred people or so came through the door to pay their respects to him. Some people drove considerable distances to make it, and some of them were people that we hadn't seen in years.

We were there, not until 8:00, but until closer to 9, just because there were still people coming through the door.

Not only did he deserve such an outpouring of love, and a visitation that was full of loud, chattering people celebrating the life of a one-of-a-kind guy…

He wouldn't have had it any other way.

epilogue.
best friends are forever.

To have ended the whole book on that note would have been way too sad. Not to mention, I don't think it's really the end of his story. A story's only over when there are no people left to tell it, and you can bet that there are a whole lot of people who are going to be telling their own Elmer stories for a very, very long time. At any rate, that isn't what I want people to know, or how I want people to walk away from this. I want people to be happy, to know that there was a very, very cool guy who lived on this earth for eighty-four wonderful years, who could make anyone smile without much work at all, who could tell a story better than anyone, who taught me everything I ever need to know to live a happy, laughter- and love-filled life.

I want people to know that it's possible to make an impression on the lives of everyone around you just by being yourself. I want people to know the stories that I was lucky enough to witness over twenty-two years of my life, that some things people might not believe are things that actually happen.

I want people to know that I wish everyone in the whole world could be lucky enough to have an Elmer.

I want people to know how grateful *I* am to have had *him*.

I'm not even half the storyteller he was, but I hope with all my heart that these snippets, these mini-snapshots of moments have made you smile, that they've made you laugh, and that they've led you to think of your own special Elmer-moments if you were lucky enough to know him personally, or that, if you didn't, you've gotten an idea of the kind of man he was, and that you've smiled and laughed just as much, perhaps thinking of someone you know.

It's really hard to believe that it's already been a year without him, but I think a big part of that is because I have the very strong suspicion that he's still hanging around, keeping tabs on me, and keeping me on my toes. His favorite song by the Beatles, "Let it Be," plays regularly on the radio (Actually, that's the *only* song by the Beatles he liked). More often than not, I spot his favorite number – any variation of the combination of 618 – popping up in all sorts of places. And every once in awhile I get a white feather that shows up, floating merrily around. I have my mom's friend to thank for that idea; she once told me that when you find a white feather, it's from someone who loves you, letting you know that they're alright. I once found a blue marble in his flower bed when I was taking care of the azalea bush before new people moved into the apartment, and then there was the New York 2011 trip, where Elmers popped up in a few different places.

Not to mention the St. Louis Cardinals won the World Series after a whole lot of speculation if they would even make the playoffs. What was more, their amazing run to the World Series was heralded by a spunky, sassy, bold little squirrel. Add on to all of that that, if there was a bigger Cardinals fan than he was, I'd be surprised, well, again. Sometimes you might just have to think.

An acorn also attacked me in the middle of the sidewalk outside of my house, despite the fact that there are no acorn-bearing trees anywhere nearby. If anyone would find it funny to pelt me with an acorn, it would have been him. He was, after all, the one who first taught me to feed the squirrels, and who also thought it was funny to aim a lemon at me across the table when he was making his lemon water at restaurants, trying to get it to squirt me. At this very moment, there's an Elmo balloon stuck and happily bobbing in the tree outside my house, and the invoice number to have my computer fixed was 2011618. Both were spotted within moments of each other.

So, even though I miss him every day, all day long, and I wish that I could just pick up the phone again and give him a call – I've thought about doing it so many times before remembering that I can't, especially when I got the news that Nate McLouth was coming back to the Pirates under a one-year contract, among many other things that I know he would have made fun of me for, but would have been just as excited about, underneath the teasing – I'm okay because I know that he's always going to be around me, even though he's not around.

Everything I Know

Batman would never leave Batgirl n the lurch.
The Skipper would never leave Gilligan marooned.
You know why?

Best friends are forever.
That might just be the most important lesson he ever taught me.

And I learned it.

Thanks for everything, Bud. Thank you for twenty-two years of love, mischief, laughter, and fun. Thank you for the memories I'll never forget, and that I'll never forget to treasure. You were, are, and always will be the best friend a girl ever could have asked for. I love you.

"You think the dead we loved ever truly leave us? You think that we don't recall them more clearly than ever in times of great trouble?"

- Albus Dumbledore,
Harry Potter and the Prisoner of Azkaban

J.K. Rowling

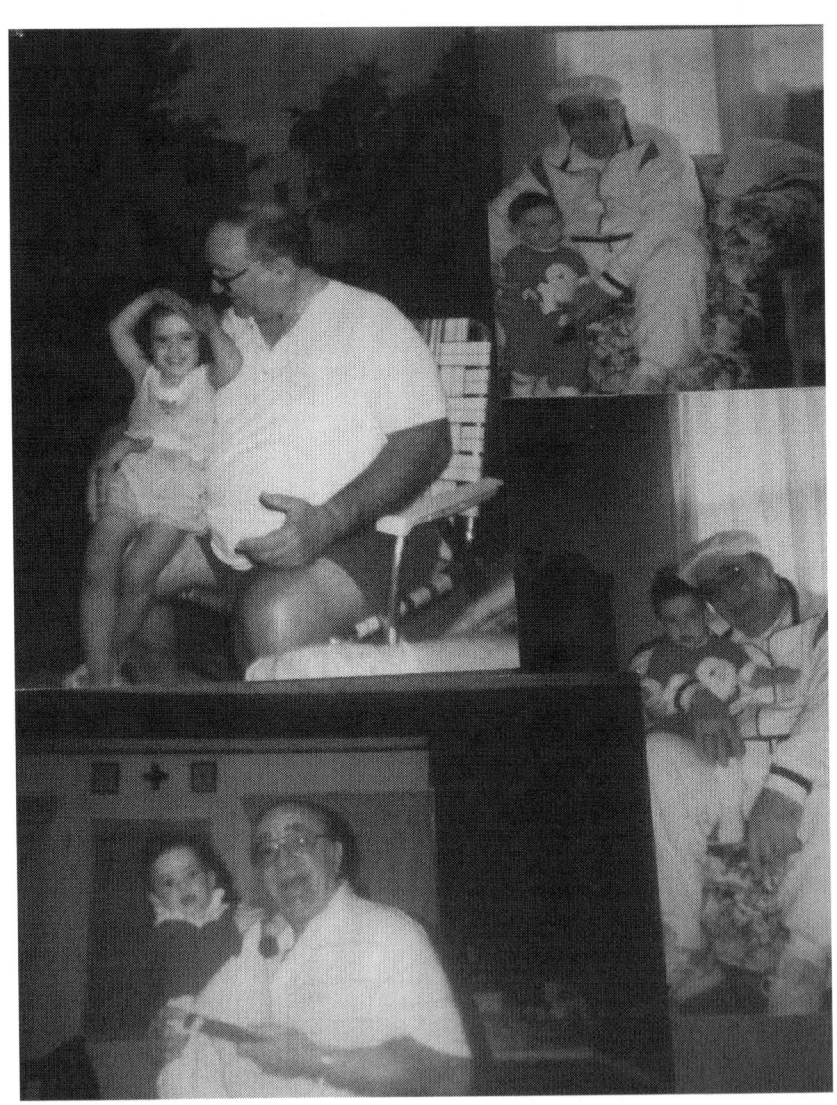

ABOUT THE AUTHOR

Megan O'Neill is a 2010 graduate of Duquesne University, and holds a B.A. in English. She is also the author of *(Baseball) Diamonds Are a Girl's Best Friend*, available on the CreateSpace eStore, through Amazon, and at Barnes & Noble's website. She is currently at work on her third and fourth books: a mystery novel, and a second baseball book.

Keep up with her on Twitter (@missmegs13), or on GoodReads (http://www.goodreads.com/missmegs13)!

11644171R00058

Made in the USA
Charleston, SC
11 March 2012